VAST UNIVERSE

Vast Universe

Extraterrestrials and Christian Revelation

Thomas F. O'Meara

$\boxed{\begin{array}{c} \text{M} \\ \hline \text{G} \end{array}}$

A Michael Glazier Book

LITURGICAL PRESS
Collegeville, Minnesota

www.litpress.org

A Michael Glazier Book published by Liturgical Press

Cover design by Ann Blattner. Photo of cosmic cloud courtesy of NASA, portrait of NGC 281.

1   2   3   4   5   6   7   8

Library of Congress Cataloging-in-Publication Data

O'Meara, Thomas F., 1935–
    Vast universe : extraterrestrials and Christian revelation / Thomas F. O'Meara.
        p.   cm.
    "A Michael Glazier book."
    Includes bibliographical references and index.
    ISBN 978-0-8146-8047-6 (alk. paper) — ISBN 978-0-8146-8048-3 (e-book)
    1. Life on other planets—Religious aspects—Christianity.
2. Extraterrestrial anthropology.   3. Theological anthropology—Christianity.   I. Title.

BR115.L54O44   2012
233—dc23   2011044770

God fixes the number of stars,
calling each by name.

—Psalm 147

Die unbegreiflich hohen Werke
Herrlich wie am ersten Tag.

The unimaginable lofty works
Magnificent, just as on that first day.

—Goethe, "Prolog im Himmel," *Faust*

"But do you really mean, sir," said Peter,
"that there could be other worlds—
all over the place, just around the corner—like that?"
"Nothing is more probable," said the Professor,
taking off his spectacles and beginning
to polish them, while he muttered to himself,
"I wonder what they do teach them at these schools."

—C. S. Lewis, *The Lion, the Witch and the Wardrobe*

Contents

Preface

Are there intelligent creatures, extraterrestrials, living on planets other than Earth? In this book a possible aspect of the universe meets the perspective of Christian revelation. The following chapters, written by a theologian, draw from what science has analyzed in stars and galaxies and recently in stars with planets.

What is the relationship of extraterrestrial peoples to what Christianity claims is a special history on Earth of life with God? Would the fact of persons on other planets banish or modify a divine being? Would it reduce the importance of Jesus? Are the galaxies of stars largely subject to evil forces? Does religion worship a divine wisdom and love that is small or one that is generous?

This book is not a new stage in the dialogue between science and religion, not a further treatment of topics from theodicy like divine causality and intervention, and not a derivation of science or revelation from each other. These pages are not an apologetics for Christianity and not a collection of old or new arguments for the existence of God.

Science and religion are different forms of knowledge about the unknown. Respectful of the sciences that disclose the reality of the universe, the following chapters wonder about good and evil, intelligence and freedom, and revelation and life as they might exist in other galaxies.

More and more planets in other solar systems are being discovered; their number gives this theme an importance, an excitement. We are at the edge of understanding the universe in a new way.

chapter one

Intelligent Beings on Distant Planets

These chapters ponder the cosmic in light of the terrestrial, the hypothetical in light of the real. They look at scientific discoveries in light of Christian revelation. Are there intelligent creatures on other planets in an almost endless universe of galaxies? Christian revelation offers no direct information about extraterrestrials. Their existence, as it becomes more and more probable, raises questions for a faith holding that God is active in the universe, questions for what our tellurian race calls "religion" and "revelation." Theological reflection finds itself drawn to inquire into extraterrestrials' relationships to God and to us.[1]

---

1. The literature on extraterrestrials is growing, and websites are valuable. See Michael Crowe, *The Extraterrestrial Life Debate 1750–1900: The Idea of a Plurality of Worlds from Kant to Lowell* (Cambridge: Cambridge University Press, 1986); Michael Crowe, *The Extraterrestrial Life Debate, Antiquity to 1915: A Source Book* (Notre Dame: University of Notre Dame Press, 2008); David Darling, *The Extraterrestrial Encyclopedia* (New York: Three Rivers, 2000); Joseph A. Angelo, *The Extraterrestrial Encyclopedia* (New York: Facts on File, 1991). There are works in French: Jean-Bruno Renard, *Les extraterrestres: Une nouvelle croyance religieuse?* (Paris: Cerf, 1988); Jean Heidmann et al., *Sommes-nous seuls dans l'univers?* (Paris: Fayard, 2000). In German: Dieter von Reeken, *Bibliographie der selbstständigen deutschsprachigen Literatur über ausserirdisches Leben, UFOs, Prä-Astronautik (1901–1986)* (Lödenscheid: Gesellschaft zur

The subject of the following speculative theology is creatures living on other planets circling their suns. They are intelligent and free. They have a cognitive openness, a capability for understanding analogies and symbolisms; they have their arts and sciences. Extraterrestrials are intelligent beings having some form of body, some matter. Beings without corporeality are in religious traditions called angels. Angels sometimes have a place, if often a slight one, in terrestrial religions. Semitic peoples from the Jews to the Persians developed a religious imagery about angelic beings, and Judaism a century or so before Jesus Christ speculated on different kinds of angels, creatures more or less without matter sent by God to perform some service for men and women. There has been discussion through the centuries on whether angels are totally spiritual. Early Christianity mentions angels as messengers but opposes any cult of angels, any involvement of human religion with powerful spirits. In a sense, Christian faith through history has addressed indirectly the possibility of extraterrestrials with its few speculations on angelic and demonic superbeings.[2]

Angels, however, are not extraterrestrials. Extraterrestrials with intellect and freedom would exist on planets in their own variations, living with many unusual forms (for Earth) of animal and vegetal life. An extraterrestrial might be quite different from terrestrial

Erforschung des UFO-Phänomens, 1987). In Italian: Giancarlo Genta, *Lonely Minds in the Universe* (New York: Copernicus Books, 2007); F. Bertola et al., eds., *Origini, l'Universo, la Vita, l'intelligenza* (Padua: Il Poligrafo, 1994).

2. See H. Bietenhard, *Die himmlische Welt im Urchristentum und Spätjudentum* (Tübingen: Mohr, 1951). Jesus is sometimes called an "angel" because he is God's messenger. In Hebrew the "el" at the end of the names of angels (e.g., Gabriel and Raphael) might indicate a Semitic reference to God, "El." Are angels extensions of the divine activity in the galaxies? The Ultimate tends to work through intermediaries. The angel is not an alternative to humans, not the rival of Jesus, and not the product of human consciousness. "Superior sphere of creation, energy radiating from the Divinity, ordained within and ordering the universe, the angelic world shines in revealed religions. The angel is present in a double way, in the procession from and in the return to God." Philippe Faure, *Les Anges* (Paris: Cerf, 1988), 120. Contrary to Margaret Wertheim, *The Pearly Gates of Cyberspace* (New York: Norton, 1999), intelligent animals living on planets are not particularly related to angels but rather to people on Earth.

animals and humans; the corporeal form might be atomic in size, or it might be composed of unusual combinations of chemicals. Regardless, distant thinking creatures in their free intelligent life would be embodied beings who would thus be in relationship to animal life.

Christian revelation does not mention intelligent creatures on other planets. Theology does not seek mythical or miraculous clues to extraterrestrials but only ponders their possibility in light of Christian beliefs. Carl Sagan wrote, "It's of interest to me that our language has not really any appropriate terms for such beings. Theological languages have terms like angels and demigods and seraphim and so on."[3] The Christian Gospel is not about angels or demigods but about the dignity and future of the human race in Jesus Christ.

Vast Universe

The universe is about thirteen and a half billion years old. It is more than ninety billion light-years across. Timothy Ferris writes, "Were the Sun a grain of sand, Earth's orbit would be an inch in radius, the solar system the size of a beach ball, and the nearest star another sand grain four miles away. Yet even on that absurdly compressed scale, the Milky Way galaxy would be a hundred thousand miles wide."[4] Around three thousand stars can be visible to Earth on a clear night. Scientists hold that there are around 125 billion galaxies, and each galaxy is calculated to have billions of stars. Recently, astronomers asked whether or not they should increase their estimate of the number of stars in the universe, stating that it is

---

3. Sagan, *The Varieties of Scientific Experience: A Personal View of the Search for God* (New York: Penguin, 2006), 103.

4. Timothy Ferris, *Seeing in the Dark* (New York: Simon and Schuster, 2002), 253. "Within 100 million light-years of earth—well within the reach of visual observers with medium-sized telescopes, and of small telescopes with CCD cameras—reside 160 groups comprising 2,500 large galaxies and perhaps 25,000 dwarf galaxies, containing something on the order of 500 trillion stars." Ibid., 261. See Nigel Henbest and Heath Couper, *The Guide to the Galaxy* (Cambridge: Cambridge University Press, 1994), 50.

possible that there are ten to twenty times as many stars as had been recently calculated.[5]

A galaxy is an aggregation of stars with a basic form held together by gravity that moves as a unit. The billions of galaxies in the universe are often in groups drawn together by gravity and other forces. In the direction of the constellation Coma Berenices, there is a cluster of three thousand galaxies. Earth's galaxy is the Milky Way, a spiral galaxy with billions of stars. This galaxy moves in association with a small group of around six to ten galaxies, and they are part of a larger cluster of thirty-one galaxies, the Local Group. This group in turn belongs to the Virgo cluster of galaxies, which is constituted by around three thousand galaxies. Although they are fifty million light-years away, they have some gravitational influence on Earth. The Andromeda Galaxy, visible to the eye even though it is two and a half million light-years away, is a larger version of our galaxy, half as big again as the Milky Way and containing twice as many stars—an estimated four hundred billion. The sun around which Earth circles was formed about five billion years ago and is located about two-thirds of the way out to the edge of our galaxy. The center of our galaxy, twenty-eight thousand light-years from Earth, is a disk with areas particularly dense with millions of stars, and it has spiral arms with star clusters, nebulae, and individual stars. Timothy Ferris illustrates the distances: "The Sun lies out in the suburbs of an average (well, larger than average) spiral galaxy in an ordinary group, which in turn resides out towards the fringes of a supercluster. If the supercluster were scaled down to cover the surface of Earth, our galaxy would be say, Boston; the Andromeda galaxy would be about the size and distance of New York City; and the brightest city light in this part of the universe, those of downtown Virgo, would be Los Angeles."[6]

Within the Milky Way, a particular cloud of stellar materials is the nebula in Orion. There stars are being born, a process that began

5. See the research of Pieter Van Dokkum mentioned by Pete Spotts in *Christian Science Monitor* (December 1, 2010).

6. Ferris, *Seeing in the Dark*, 254. "Today polls show that roughly half the population of Europe and America believes that extraterrestrial beings are out there." Seth Shostak and Alex Barnett, *Cosmic Company: The Search for Life in the Universe* (Cambridge: Cambridge University Press, 2003), 1.

about four million years ago and reached a climax about three hundred thousand years ago. Robert O'Dell writes, "All of the stars there [in Orion] have associated circumstellar disks, which means that all of them have the building blocks of planets. Rich clusters like the Orion Nebula Cluster are thought to be the prototypes for formation of most stars. What goes on there is probably what has gone on in most other stars."[7] The great number of stars, their various kinds and ages, and the birth of countless stars in the future make solar systems with planets more than a possibility. Even in the Milky Way alone, they might be numerous.[8]

Discoveries

In 1991 astronomers Alexander Wiszczan and Dale Frail concluded that a planetary companion was orbiting a distant star. In 1995 two scientists at the University of Geneva discovered the first exoplanet. Exoplanets are discerned by observing dips in starlight as planets cross in front of their home star or by wobbles they induce near it.

In recent decades, a robotic telescope on Palomar Mountain near San Diego, Sleuth, concluded a lengthy search for planets in our galaxy of star-suns and found twenty. To the north of San Francisco, a radio telescope with 350 dishes is being set up; the Allen Telescope Array has as one of its main purposes the search for life in outer space. A new telescope in Europe has begun the examination of 120,000 stars. The "Planet Hunters" at San Francisco State University discovered early exoplanets, while a team at the University of California at Berkeley has discovered 150 planets; they have found

7. C. Robert O'Dell, *The Orion Nebula: Where Stars Are Born* (Cambridge, MA: Harvard University Press, 2003), 154.

8. "Whatever the case—whether the Milky Way abounds with intelligent life, or whether we are its sole example—the Galaxy has already accomplished a major feat: it has given birth to intelligent life." Ken Croswell, *The Alchemy of the Heavens: Searching for Meaning in the Milky Way* (New York: Doubleday, 1995), 260. See also Amir D. Aczel, *Probability 1: Why There Must Be Intelligent Life in the Universe* (New York: Harcourt Brace and Company, 1998).

one star with similarities to our sun and with five planets.[9] Kepler, a telescope in space, will monitor 150,000 stars in the constellation Cygnus over four years by measuring the dimming caused by a planet crossing in front of the host star. The Kepler team recently published a provisional list of 1,200 stars thought to be harboring planets; it found a solar system with six planets circling a star about two thousand light-years away from us. A team using telescopes in Hawaii, Chile, Australia, and California are monitoring two thousand stars, and they have found over a hundred planets. Planets within one hundred light-years of Earth could provide sufficient light for advanced scientific instruments to analyze a planet's atmosphere and search for by-products of life. Since 1995, over six hundred planets have been found, moving at various distances around some 380 stars. Even as sophisticated searching instruments, using light and radio waves, seek out planets near other suns, some planets have been found by amateur astronomers. To date, many of the planets discovered seem not to be conducive to life because they are too close to their suns. Most of these exoplanets are large, on the scale of Saturn, although recently one or two have been discovered that are on the scale of Earth. If only one planet out of every 150,000 contained life, there would be a million worlds with life in the Milky Way. Would not some of them hold intelligent life?

Scientists have begun to speculate on the conditions for exoplanets to provide apt conditions for civilizations. "Circumstellar habitable zones" in the universe are zones where conditions are right for life. They are, for instance, narrow disks around a star where

---

9. The European Southern Observatory hopes that its High Accuracy Radial Velocity Planet Search will be "the world's foremost exoplanet hunter." "Planets of Other Stars," in *Astronomica*, ed. Fred Watson (Elanora, Australia: Millenium House, 2007), 156–60. African nations plan a radio array with three thousand antennas to seek out new exoplanets. "Afrika blickt in das All: Der Kontinent will ein millardenteures Teleskop bauen," *Süddeutsche Zeitung* 20 (January, 2010): 16. See also Robert Irion, "The Planet Hunters," *Smithsonian* (October 2006): 40–45; Timothy Ferris, "Worlds Apart," *National Geographic* (December 2009): 91; Rudolf Dvorak, *Extrasolar Planets: Formation, Detection and Dynamics* (Weinheim: Wiley-VCH, 2008); and "The New Universe," special edition, *National Geographic* (Washington, DC: National Geographic Society, 2010): 98.

temperatures on the planet are moderate enough for water to exist in liquid form.[10] Ken Croswell summarizes:

> During the 1990s, astronomers for the first time established that the universe at large does indeed possess the four basic astronomical ingredients for life. Prior to that decade, astronomers already knew that stars forge life-giving elements like carbon and oxygen, and that giant galaxies such as the Milky Way sculpt these life-giving elements and recycle them into new star systems, and that many stars generate the abundant light and warmth which life requires. Now astronomers know that the fourth and final ingredient also exists: planets around other stars.[11]

10. See James Kasting, *How to Find a Habitable Planet* (Princeton, NJ: Princeton University Press, 2010); Victoria S. Meadows, "Planetary Environmental Signature for Habitability and Life," in *Exoplanets: Detection, Formation, Properties, Habitability*, ed. John W. Mason (New York: Praxis, 2008), 259–84; Jean Heidmann, "Habitable Zones in the Universe," in *Extraterrestrial Intelligence* (Cambridge: Cambridge University Press, 1995); C. B. Cosmovici, Stuart Bowyer, and Dan Werthimer, *Astronomical and Biochemical Origins and the Search for Life in the Universe* (Bologna: Editrice Compositori, 1997); SETI Institute, *How Might Life Evolve on Other Worlds?* (Englewood, CO: Teacher Ideas Press, 1995); John Billingham, ed., *Life in the Universe* (Cambridge, MA: MIT Press, 1981), 209–332; David Darling, "Galactic Habitable Zones," in *The Extraterrestrial Encyclopedia*, 179–81.

11. Ken Croswell, *Planet Quest: The Epic Discovery of Alien Solar Systems* (New York: The Free Press, 1997), 246. See Steven J. Dick, *Extraterrestrial Life and Our World View at the Turn of the Millennium* (Washington, DC: Smithsonian Institute, 2000). There are writings on other kinds of universes that are not visible or detectable at the present. "The *observed* Universe, with its three dimensions, four forces and finite size, may not only be just a small part of an infinite whole but an unrepresentative part at that." John D. Barrow, *The Infinite Book: A Short Guide to the Boundless, Timeless and Endless* (New York: Vintage Books, 2005), 143. These worlds may be few or numerous or nonexistent, and their relationships to matter, light, and time are yet to be explained. Multiple universes or parallel universes can easily slip into the genre of science fiction. Whether or not there are universes utterly different and unknown, the universe that is explored from Earth through light and radio waves is nonetheless the subject of these pages. For reading on parallel universes, see Brian Greene, *The Hidden Reality: Parallel Universes and the Deep Laws of the Cosmos* (New York: Knopf, 2011).

The search for planets is a search for life and for intelligent life: for material beings with the ability to live through change, to create new environments, to enjoy abstract thinking, and to pursue culture and religion.

Ideas about the possibility of an active search for extraterrestrials led to the establishment of SETI (Search for Extraterrestrial Intelligence) Institute. This institute's main project became operational on October 12, 1992, as the giant antenna at Arecibo, Puerto Rico, turned to the sky to receive radio transmissions from other civilizations. SETI monitors incoming radio waves from stars and looks for patterns in their frequencies that might indicate a signal deliberately sent by an extraterrestrial intelligence, as contrasted with regular signals from natural sources. The main telescopes used by SETI are in Puerto Rico and Great Britain. This enterprise has expanded through other institutes and amateur astronomers, because SETI allows people at home to analyze their data. Over several decades, SETI has examined fewer than one thousand stars for faint radio signals, but that number should grow to a million in the next twenty-five years. The project estimates that ten thousand civilizations are transmitting in our galaxy alone. The lack of success to date points to the limitations in Earth's technology and to the gulfs imposed by space and time.[12]

12. See Paul Davies, *The Eerie Silence: Renewing Our Search for Alien Intelligence* (Boston: Houghton Mifflin Harcourt, 2010); J. H. Wolfe et al., "SETI—The Search for Extraterrestrial Intelligence: Plans and Rationale," in *Life in the Universe*, ed. John Billingham, 391–418; Seth Shostak, "Closing in on E.T.," *Sky and Telescope* (November 2010): 22–25. On the SETI League, see H. Paul Shuch, "Amateur SETI," *Sky and Telescope* (November 2010): 29; Cyril Ponnamperum and A. G. W. Cameron, eds., *Interstellar Communication: Scientific Perspectives* (Boston: Houghton Mifflin Company, 1974); Fernando Ballesteros, *E. T. Talk: How Will We Communicate with Intelligent Life on Other Worlds?* (New York: Springer, 2010). "There are roughly fifty civilizations in the entire Galaxy that are likely to be engaged in trying to communicate using the means presently available to us on earth. Assuming a 500-year 'radio window' and given the fact that humans have had the ability to receive and broadcast interstellar message for about 50 years, this suggests that there are about five radio-capable civilizations that are marginally behind us in their technology and about forty-five that are more advanced. . . . Fifty 'radio-stage' civilizations

Probabilities

Frank Drake pioneered the enterprise of thinking about other inhabited planets. In 1961 he established an equation that looks at *probabilities.* In a galaxy, what is the percentage of stars permitting the formation of planets? What is the very minimal percentage of planets hospitable to life? What is a minimal percentage of those planets that would have intelligent life? The Drake Equation is N $= R \cdot f_p \cdot n_e \cdot f_l \cdot f_i \cdot f_c \cdot L$.[13] The number of civilizations that could communicate with each other (N) would be the product of seven estimates: R, the rate at which stars form in one galaxy (the Milky Way, in our case); f_p, the fraction of stars that have planets around them; n_e, the number of planets per star that are capable of sustaining life; f_l, the fraction of suitable planets whose forms of life actually evolve; f_i, the fraction of those where life evolves into intelligent life; f_c, the fraction of those who develop the technology to communicate out into other galaxies; and L, the fraction of planetary civilizations whose history overlaps with ours. When one assumes the smallest percentage at each stage, the Milky Way alone is so populated with stars that the likelihood of intelligent life on other planets with the ability to communicate across the galaxy is considerable. Only a fraction of habitable planets would have some form of life, and, further, the fraction of those on which intelligent life has evolved might be small. Commentators on this topic project that if, on average, a civilization endures for between one thousand and one million years, the number of communicating civilizations in our galaxy is between one

---

equate to one for roughly every 8 billion stars." David Darling, "Drake Equation," in *The Extraterrestrial Encyclopedia* (New York: Three Rivers: 2000), 112.

13. For an exposition of the Drake Equation, see Frank D. Drake, "Extraterrestrial Intelligence: The Significance of the Search," in *Carl Sagan's Universe*, ed. Yervant Terzian and Elizabeth Bilson (Cambridge: Cambridge University Press, 1997), 87–97; James Kasting, "The Drake Equation Revisited: The Search for Extraterrestrial Intelligence," in *How to Find a Habitable Planet*, 290–95; Steve Nadis, "How Many Civilizations Lurk in the Cosmos?" *Astronomy* (April 2010), 24–29. For a critique of various arguments for the probability of extraterrestrials from the point of view of logic, see André Kukla, *Extraterrestrials: A Philosophical Perspective* (New York: Rowman and Littlefield, 2010).

thousand and one million. Perhaps advanced beings would inhabit one in every four hundred thousand star systems among billions.

The Drake Equation does not give a proof for technological civilizations in the galaxy, but it encourages and directs research by future generations concerning the way the universe probably actually is. Drake's equation has received considerable acceptance in the scientific community and has been of service for almost fifty years.

Gulfs

Space is the first gulf. Earth and other stars exist far apart. Millions of light-years separate galaxies. The light of the stars seen at nighttime left their sources for Earth at the time of Plato or in the age of the dinosaurs. Contact by light or radio waves takes long periods of time. Contact by travel is difficult to imagine. The great difficulty confronting voyagers to the stars stems from the enormous distances of the stars themselves. Many scientists note that even the stars nearest to Earth are extremely distant. The spacecraft sent by NASA to explore planets like Saturn and Uranus would require eighty thousand years to reach Alpha Centauri, the closest star (other than the Sun) to Earth. Traveling fast requires great amounts of energy and money to research new technological approaches; a velocity of ten percent of the speed of light vastly exceeds the fastest spacecraft ever launched or imagined by terrestrial science. Even if one could reduce the traveler to light or matter, journeys might be blocked by the structure of the universe in terms of light and relativity. "The challenges of interstellar travel are enormous—perhaps so enormous that its critics are right, and no civilization will ever be able to achieve it, thereby explaining why our Galaxy could abound with intelligent species we have never met."[14]

14. Croswell, *Planet Quest*, 245. Carl Sagan wrote, "It will not be we who reach Alpha Centauri and the other nearby stars. It will be species very like us but with more of our strength and fewer of our weaknesses, a species returned to circumstances more like those for which it was originally evolved, more confident, farseeing, capable and prudent—the sorts of beings we would want to represent us in a Universe that, for all we know, is filled with species much older, much more powerful, and very different. The vast distances that separate

A second gulf is that of time. Other civilizations would have their own times, their own histories. The life span of civilizations is not easily determined and can occur over hundreds of millions of years before or after the present time on Earth. Cultures emerge and then die out, and this occurs over billions of years. Ferris notes these temporal distances: "The first gulf is the amount of time it takes signals to travel between contemporaneous civilizations. If, as some of the optimistic SETI scientists estimate, there are 10,000 worlds in the Milky Way galaxy today, the average time required to send a one-way message to one's nearest neighbor—across the back fence, so to speak—is on the order of 1,000 years."[15] If extraterrestrials had sent to Earth a signal ten or twenty thousand years ago, it would have arrived amid humans concerned with the problems of an ice age. Even if civilizations stay on the air for millions of years, the odds are not high that they will overlap with civilizations in one galaxy. Isaac Asimov wrote,

> Suppose that each civilization that comes into being endures only a comparatively short time and then comes to an end. That would mean that if we could examine all the inhabitable planets in the Universe, we might find that on a large number of them civilization has not yet arisen, and that on an even larger number civilization has arisen, but has already become extinct. Only on a very few planets would we find a civilization that has arisen so recently that it has not yet had time to become extinct. The briefer the duration of civilizations, the less likely we are to encounter a world on which the civilization has come and not yet gone.[16]

the stars are providential. Beings and worlds are quarantined from one another. The quarantine is lifted only for those with sufficient self-knowledge and judgment to have safely traveled from star to star." *Pale Blue Dot: A Vision of the Human Future in Space* (New York: Random House, 1994), 398. See also Sagan, "Extraterrestrial Folklore: Implications of the Evolution of Religion," in *The Varieties of Scientific Experience*, 125–45.

15. Timothy Ferris, "Interstellar Spaceflight: Can We Travel to Other Stars?" in *The Best American Science Writing 2000* (New York: Ecco Press, 2000), 178–92.

16. Isaac Asimov, *Extraterrestrial Civilizations* (New York: Crown Publications, 1979), 189.

Do the majority of extraterrestrial societies belong to the past? Or to the future?

The star cluster Pleiades in the constellation Taurus contains hundreds of young stars that formed from a natal gas cloud expanding about one hundred million years ago. Slowly, the protostars separate from each other and move to maturity. Does that maturity involve the production of planets? How long are the lifetimes of their civilizations (if they have any)? Chet Raymo reminds us of galactic history: "A hundred generations of stars lived and died in the Milky Way Galaxy before the sun was born, a hundred generations of stars turning hydrogen into the stuff of future planets."[17] Civilizations with a million years of history could have already come to the end of God's plan for the historical stages of their social existence. With all their achievements, they have come and gone. Earth's human civilization has had ability to communicate widely for only five thousand years and has had the ability to communicate electronically for only a little over a century. Still, because of the number of stars, there could be planetary civilizations able to be contacted even if only a small percentage of them have been flourishing over the past million years.[18]

New Realities

Learning from science, this book considers religion and faith. Christian theology is not, however, primarily about the existence of a God—that is presumed—but about God's plans and relationships

17. Chet Raymo, *Soul of the Night* (Cambridge, MA: Cowley, 2005), 84.

18. "Carl Sagan suggested that in the Milky Way [there are] a million. Drake is more modest and estimates 10,000 technological civilizations through the Milky Way. Our nearest neighbors will be 500 to 1,000 light-years distant." Shostak and Barnett, *Cosmic Company*, 133. See also David Koerner, *Here Be Dragons: The Scientific Quest for Extraterrestrial Life* (Oxford: Oxford University Press, 2000); on the issue of visitations from extraterrestrials with their kinds of life, see Ben Zuckerman and Michael H. Hart, *Extraterrestrials—Where are They?* (Cambridge: Cambridge University Press, 1995); Stephen Webb, *If the Universe Is Teeming with Aliens . . . Where Is Everybody? Fifty Solutions to the Fermi Paradox and the Problem of Extraterrestrial Life* (New York: Praxis, 2002).

with creatures. The being at the source of the universe bestows further modalities of its power and love; they are what religions call "revelation," "grace," "salvation," or "divine presence." A theologian would not presume to decide whether there are other intelligent beings in the universe. Apart from a few allusions to angels or demons, Christian revelation does not mention the relationship of God to other intelligent creatures. Extraterrestrials with intellect and freedom might exist on planets in various forms amid countless species of animal and vegetal life. Christian revelation, however, is specifically about people on Earth.[19]

Christian stances that oppose extraterrestrials usually emphasize an exalted distance for God, the sinfulness of any free being, and a miraculous uniqueness of Jesus. There are Catholic and Orthodox devotions that make Jesus king of the Sun, planets, and stars, but they are stating through religious rhetoric and poetry the drama of the risen Christ. His special role on Earth is not compromised by other intelligent creatures. Extraterrestrials do not impinge upon the traditional theology of the incarnation of the Word of God in Jesus: it takes place on Earth. Ted Peters, a pioneer in considering these issues, writes, "What is misleading here is the assumption that the Christian religion is fragile, that it is so fixed upon its orientation to human beings centered on earth than an experience with extraterrestrial beings would shatter it. An alleged earth centrism

---

19. There are critics of the reality of extraterrestrials who draw on their particular Christian theologies. For Benjamin Wiker, the search for other civilizations has been "dismal." "Alien Ideas: Christianity and the Search for Extraterrestrial Life," *Crisis* (November 2002): 30. See also George Basalla, *Civilized Life in the Universe: Scientists on Intelligent Extraterrestrials* (Oxford: Oxford University Press, 2006). If there are only intelligent creatures on Earth, that does not imply that God is narrow or second rate. Wentzel van Huyssteen argues from a religious point of view that it is God's plan that we be alone in the universe, that men and women are unique as the "image" of God. From a religious point of view, what we see and believe on Earth is all there is. See van Huyssteen, *Alone in the World: Human Uniqueness in Science and Theology* (Grand Rapids: Eerdmans, 2006), xiv–xviii. See also Ted Peters, "Fundamentalist Literature," in *Science, Theology, and Ethics* (Burlington, VT: Ashgate, 2003), 129–34; Bruce M. Jakosky, *Science, Society and the Search for Life in the Universe* (Tuscon: University of Arizona Press, 2006), 117–21.

renders Christianity vulnerable." Peters introduces an alternative: "To the contrary, I find that when the issue of beings on other worlds has been raised it has been greeted positively. . . . I advocate *exotheology*—that is, speculation on the theological significance of extraterrestrial life."[20] For Christian theology the probability of extraterrestrials is not completely new. Surprisingly, theologians from the past nineteen centuries have offered ideas about intelligent creatures on the stars (as we will see in later chapters). Theologians in Alexandria, Paris, Florence, and Boston have not been afraid of affirming extraterrestrials.[21] A few books on science treating extraterrestrials have references to religion; many have none. Books on "religion and science" may mention God as a mental construct, an appendage to the universe, or an antiquated myth. Frequently when a scientist mentions religion, it is not faith-in-revelation that is the subject but the approach and content of a philosophy, a view of God that is metaphysical or mechanistic. Theodicies and metaphysics, deism and agnosticism, however, are cold and spare; revelation is always about more. The concern of most human religions and especially of Christianity is a further special presence of God. Organized religion has been accompanied by fears of scientific discoveries, while the rise of science was accompanied by the dismissal of religion. Today science and religion are recognizing some similarities and a relationship between them. There can be theology without dogmatism and science without agnosticism. Scientists observe that two central dynamics further the search for extraterrestrial intelligence: astronomy and religion. Space and spirit endeavors are both gateways, even if they

20. Ted Peters, "Exotheology: Speculations on Extraterrestrial Life," in *Science, Theology, and Ethics*, 121f. See also Peters, "Astrotheology and the ETI Myth," *Theology and Science* 7 (2009): 3–29; Charles L. Harper, ed., *Spiritual Information: 100 Perspectives on Science and Religion* (Philadelphia: Templeton Foundation Press, 2005); and Charles L. Harper, "Annual Banquet Address," *Bulletin of the North American Paul Tillich Society* 35 (2009): 4–5l.

21. To offer perspectives from Christianity on the galaxies is to imply that other faiths and religions on Earth would have their own dialogues with wider worlds. Hinduism and Buddhism might have their perspectives, as would the religious mentalities of human beings in earlier times. See Giancarlo Genta, "The Religious Perspective," in *Lonely Minds in the Universe* (New York: Copernicus Books, 2007), 23–36.

are not the same. They arise from the mists of ancient reflections to serve as guides for understanding humanity broadly and deeply. Both science and religion have entered a new time as they pass beyond isolation and anxiety, beyond mental constructs and words. Science and theology will find creativity and colleagueship. This enterprise challenges Christian faith.

Christian theology considers in faith and reticence how a free, intelligent person on a planet far from the center of its own galaxy is related to a cosmic Source or loving Parent. Theodore Hesburgh wrote thirty years ago, "What reflects God most is intelligence and freedom, not matter. Why suppose that He did not create the most of what reflects Him the best? He certainly made a lot of matter. Why not more intelligence, more free beings, who alone can seek and know him? . . . Finding others than ourselves would mean knowing Him better."[22] A wide cosmos does not raise doubts about a true God, for the God above god (as philosophers and mystics have put it) is not glorified by negative and small religiosity. Neither humanity nor divinity implies isolation. Among beings with intelligence and freedom, there would be some slight similarity to Earth. Intelligent beings on different planets would have an analogous communality in knowledge and science, arts and communication.[23] The opposite

---

22. Hesburgh, "Foreword," in Philip Morrison et al., eds., *The Search for Extraterrestrial Intelligence (SETI)* (NASA, 1977), vii. In a recent survey, eighty-two percent of Catholics said that the discovery of extraterrestrial life would not threaten their faith. Ted Peters, "Peters ETI Religious Crisis Survey of 2008," Center for Theology and the Natural Sciences, Graduate Theology Union, August 15, 2008.

23. Some directions in theology and the philosophy of religion might find a dynamic view of life in the cosmos to be a liberation. Religion is not just texts and terminologies. Faith contemplates the universe and the persons in it, and science and faith are both involved with the question and the reality of the breadth of the universe and not mainly with mathematical or other mental forms. Seeking the divine in the extraterrestrial, theology would go beyond the Cartesian and Kantian revolutions with their declining audiences, beyond two hundred years of expositions of how the knowing subject forms and limits religion. Postmodernism in philosophy and religion still withdraws more into mental forms and words, moving away from extrahuman realities. Catholicism is essentially involved in realities. The incarnation of Christianity and the sacramentality of Catholicism are about the visual, the aesthetic, the real.

of seeking God in life and in the world is not emptiness but an ideo-
logical system, whether of religion or science. God is not a puzzle but
a depth, inaccessible because so rich and different. Today theology
aims not at propositions but realities; it strives not for reduction but
expansion.

Telescopes and radio arrays are being planned and built to go
further into the mystery of the real. Chet Raymo writes, "We are
caught up in an evolving universe we only partly understand, illumi-
nated by a flame of life that reaches into the deep crustal rocks of the
earth and perhaps to distant planets. We may take this astonishing
story on the word of the scientists, but if we are attentive to what
they say—and imaginative and courageous—we too will feel the
terrifying, exhilarating wind of primeval fire blowing through our
lives."[24] The Christian view of the dignity of the human person made
in the image of God, the call of life in the future, and the interplay
of knowing and loving assist Earth in making a contribution to a
wider understanding of the cosmos.

This book is led by discoveries in the universe. The history of
philosophy and theology gives examples—Albertus Magnus, Friedrich Schelling, Pierre Teilhard de Chardin—of how science stimu-
lates Christian reflection to find new paradigms and insights.[25] What

24. Raymo, "Let Me Begin This Celebration of Life," *Notre Dame Magazine*
(Spring 2010): 24.

25. Modern philosophy itself began in a quest for a system that was universal, a
kind of unified field theory. After 1795, the writings of F. W. J. Schelling related
the powers of the self, the history of religion, and the forms of art to nature
explored by the new sciences of chemistry and electromagnetism. In all these
there was occurring the one "odyssey of the spirit," where nature was spirit
made visible. The inner powers of God retain mystery and depth even as they
lead to the unfolding of the universe of being and the history of religion. See
Joseph L. Esposito, *Schelling's Idealism and Philosophy of Nature* (Lewisburg:
Bucknell University Press, 1977); Emilio Brito, *La Création selon Schelling*
(Leuven: Leuven University Press, 1987).

emerges is also a new look at Christian revelation, at the fundamental realities of what is believed. If being and revelation and grace come to worlds other than Earth, that modifies in a modest way Christian self-understanding. It is not a question of adding or subtracting but of seeing what is basic in a new way. The being of a credible God, plurality in God, creation, incarnation, revelation, love, and community find in the following chapters a new tonality. The following chapters on other intelligent civilizations in light of Christian perspectives look at the religious framework of personhood, freedom, evil, history, and revelation from God; at divine plans and presences in the times of galactic worlds; at Jesus and incarnation; and at special destinies in history and time. The pages have their own approach: they prefer the real to the devout, the intelligible to the contradictory, seeing to willing, process to decline, variety to monoformity.

Throughout history human beings on Earth have looked in new directions and crossed distant boundaries. The explorer, the scientist, and the artist go forward into what is unknown. Basic reflections on religion encourage the sending of sound and light out into the stars. Christian revelation can encourage an appreciation of a vast universe and a lengthy future. Today, through websites of searching organizations, a computer at home can bring up a photograph of a field of bright stars, one of which is circled: it has a planet.

chapter two

Extraterrestrials amid Nature, Grace, and Sin

Are there intelligent creatures on planets far away? There are billions of suns in one galaxy: perhaps not a few of them offer light and warmth for planets with life where societies of science and art flourish. Civilizations on unusual planets might be numerous in the universe, just as species of animals and plants are numerous on Earth, where there are three hundred kinds of squid and twelve thousand varieties of ants. There might be several hundred intelligent societies in each galaxy, and there are billions of galaxies. Some scientists think that, once life originates, the evolution of complex and intelligent life forms of some sort is likely, if not inevitable.[1]

Human beings have long known that reality is more than what their knowledge at any moment can grasp. Tens of thousands of years ago, painters sought to depict on the walls of caves the depth and force of animals. To reflect on the possible conditions of unknown beings is not presumptuous for Christian theology. As search

---

1. See Guillermo Gonzalez and Jay Richards, "SETI and the Unraveling of the Copernican Principle," in *The Privileged Planet: How Our Place in the Cosmos Is Designed for Discovery* (Washington, DC: Regnery, 2004).

instruments let the material forms of the galaxies show themselves, so theology contemplates unexpected implications of existence and life. There can be a believer's phenomenology of the universe.

The Triad of Religion

Christian revelation addresses peoples and communities as they relate to God. While planets in distant galaxies would have their own ecosystems and histories, their own networks of social forms and achievements in art and technology, they would also have their own religions. For a religious consideration of extraterrestrials, three topics are basic: (1) the knowing and free person, (2) the person's relationship to God, and (3) the person's contacts with sin and evil. This triad is the fundamental realm explored by Christian faith. Thinking about it on other planets is an open framework and not a doctrine.

Religions are not mainly about a deity's existence. They ponder and celebrate relationships of people to God; they believe in a revelation from and about God; they speak about empowerment from God for good and about the injuries and deaths coming from evil and sin. To consider this religious triad is to consider the dialectic of the divine and the human, the spiritual and the historical, the mystical and the sacramental. The following pages look at each of these three—the person, God's presence, sin—as fundamental in possible extraterrestrial lives.

Variety in Intelligent Life

The Big Bang points to the possibility of an indefinite number of planets with different properties, some of which are suitable for intelligences engaging their worlds.[2] Carl Sagan observed, "There is no reason to think that there is only one path to intelligent life. The

2. See Jean-Bruno Renard on evil intentions, transcendence, revelation, messianism, milleniarism, and technology as aspects of "aliens," in *Les extraterrestres: Une nouvelle croyance religieuse?* (Paris: Cerf, 1988), 89–117. See also David Darling, "Extraterrestrial Intelligence," in *The Extraterrestrial Encyclopedia*

selective advantage of intelligence is clearly high."[3] For Christian faith and theology, the nature of other intelligent creatures is open. For galaxies with hundreds of millions of solar systems, it is likely that the divine being sets forth a diversity of intelligent creatures. The universe might follow a range of possible evolutionary paths. Women and men through history and culture produce a variety of psychologies and anthropologies, while epochal styles influence painting and literature. Civilizations on other planets may have forms of science and art that have not occurred to us. Contrary to the dramas of science fiction, they would not live amid large versions of Greek temples, wear impenetrable medieval armor, or fly in airplanes constructed to look like pterodactyls. On other planets, thousands of light-years away, a culture might exist that now in the twenty-first century would be unimaginable to us.

While the universe increasingly suggests the possibility of varied ways of life, including intelligent life, the field of bioastronomy seeks patterns amenable to life. Scientists discuss unusual life-forms like plasma life, life in solid hydrogen, radiant life, and life in neutron stars.[4] "Extremophiles" are a varied group of organisms that thrive in harsh environments intolerable to virtually all other creatures. Since the late 1960s, scientists have discovered hundreds of extremophile species on Earth. They can survive scalding water, subzero temperatures, extreme pressures and density, or aridity; they can withstand

---

(New York: Three Rivers: 2000), 141–49; Stuart Clark, "ET IQ," in *Life on Other Worlds and How to Find It* (New York: Praxis, 2000), 117–27.

3. Sagan, *The Varieties of Scientific Experience: A Personal View of the Search for God* (New York: The Penguin Press, 2006), 112.

4. See Gonzalez and Richards, *The Privileged Planet*; Ben Zuckerman and Michael H. Hart, *Extraterrestrials: Where Are They?* (Cambridge: Cambridge University Press, 1995); Christian de Duve, *Life Evolving: Molecules, Mind, and Meaning* (Oxford: Oxford University Press, 2002); Ben Bova, *Faint Echoes, Distant Stars: The Science and Politics of Finding Life beyond Earth* (New York: William Morrow, 2004); Steven J. Dick, *The Biological Universe: The Twentieth Century Extraterrestrial Life Debate and the Limits of Science* (Cambridge: Cambridge University Press, 1996); "Astrobiology," in *Astronomica*, ed. Fred Watson (Elanora Heights, Australia: Millennium House, 2007), 160–63; Paul Davies, "Weird Extremophiles," in *The Eerie Silence: Renewing Our Search for Alien Intelligence* (Boston: Houghton Miflin Harcourt, 2010), 47–51.

radiation and live on methane without oxygen and sunlight. Cannot life and intelligent life exist in quite unexpected forms? Scientists are asking what life would be like in galaxies with different forms of cosmic forces. Neville Brown explores constants and dynamics in the possible formation of forms of life. "Life as we thus far observe it displays a peculiarly insistent tendency, much discouragement notwithstanding, to evolve towards more complex forms which should tend *inter alia* to achieve high consciousness levels. The outreach these forms are liable to essay may or may not be successful in drawing near to Godliness in any very tangible sense. Nevertheless, they may play a signal role binding collective consciousness more tightly within the kingdom of Life."[5] Other civilizations may have originated in the same area of star birth that gave rise to us; or existing in regions far away, they might have remarkable forms of life.

We should set aside the standard Hollywood convention that extraterrestrials look just like us. Terrestrial processes leading to the human race might have happened thousands or millions of other times in the history of our galaxy. Speaking of "starfolk," Sagan imagines federations of galaxies where vast amounts of information are held collectively.[6] Intelligent extraterrestrials in forms distinct from those of Earth might enjoy a social life that has little temporality or history: their personal and religious life might be timeless. Their natural lives might be brief, or one person might live for centuries. Technologies might never be used for gain or conquest. They might emphasize characteristics of God that elude religions on Earth. These and many other issues are open. If on other planets there are beings endowed with intelligence and free will, all have been or will be created according to plans by which the divine mind lets nature, cosmic forces, and persons exist. Cosmic multitudes point to a richness at their source.

---

5. Neville Brown, *Engaging the Cosmos: Astronomy, Philosophy, and Faith* (Brighton, UK: Sussex Academic Press, 2006), 308f.

6. Carl Sagan, *Carl Sagan's Cosmic Connection*, produced by Jerome Agel (Cambridge: Cambridge University Press, 2000), 257f., 238; see Jan Narveson, "Martians and Morals: How to Treat an Alien," in *Extraterrestrials: Science and Alien Intelligence*, ed. Edward Regis (Cambridge: Cambridge University Press, 1985), 245–66.

Modes of Divine Presence

Galaxies are matter, gasses, elements, and heat caught up by gravity. Intelligence and spirit are much more. Is to be a creation of God a neutral state, one composed solely of physical and psychological forces? Or does life have an orientation toward a further fulfillment? Religion believes that there is more within and beyond intelligence, and yet, the color-filled galaxies with their suns and planets are the backdrop to intelligence. Created intellect and freedom invite and allow God's love to relate to creatures in ways of intimacy and love. Other possible civilizations have a common cause in God and a communitarian destiny with the divine.

Since the Middle Ages, the term "supernatural" has referred to a realm of being above the atoms and laws of the universe: a manner of being human not only in terms of science and art but in areas of love and service.[7] Christian faith holds that God silently but really touches men and women in a special way. Senses and sensors do not record that divine presence, but it is real, although invisible. Beyond the basic gift of existence, religion affirms further realms. Those interior modes of life—Jesus calls them the "kingdom of God" and early Christians named them "life in the Spirit"—give a fundamental revelation that God is not only cause but parent and friend. A special activity of God, "grace," touches all of human life, reaching from politics to mysticism and lying beneath areas as diverse as liturgy and ministry to the sick.[8] Faith is not simply Hebrew or English words about religion implanted in human minds. Faith is a way of knowing, of living with an intangible reality. God is not only the creator who fashions a distinct world of beings but also a person who gives a deeper mode of life that lasts into the future. What is most basic

7. Aquinas, *Summa Theologiae* I, 1, 1 (Turin: Marietti, 1952). All translations from works of Thomas Aquinas into English are by the author.

8. Already in 1952 Domenico Grasso wrote, "Knowledge of extraterrestrials would help us penetrate the wisdom of the plans of God and the evil of sin. If they live in a state of justice they would not have committed original sin, and we would see the immensity of all that was lost by our ancestors through sin. In the case of a redemption like ours we would see the special love of God for us in terms of a further experience of this love." "La Teologia e la pluralità dei mondi abitati," *Civiltà Cattolica* 193 (1952): 265.

in religion is the affirmation of some contact by God within and yet beyond human nature.

Do intelligent creatures always receive some special life and information from God? Occasionally? Rarely? Are beings on other planets called to their own special relationship with God? Through the centuries Christian theologians have asked whether there could be forms of intelligent life open to special relationships with God but content without them.[9] This is a theoretical question aimed at delineating human nature amid grace and sin. In past or future spans of a hundred million years, another planet's intelligent beings may find in their world a happy, natural life and no more; they may have in their psychological and biological energies no aspiration to life after death and no longing for fulfillment from beyond. Intelligent creatures might be free of natural disasters on their planet, from illnesses and most suffering, and yet not think of immortality. They might expect nothing beyond a peaceful span and cessation of life.

The creation of galaxies is one mode of divine action; an intimate love for creatures of intelligence is another. On Earth, revelation and grace are believed to be the mission and ministry of the divine Trinity through Word and Spirit. Even they represent only a few facets of the divine life. Roch Kereszty concludes, "Considering the consistency and unity of what we already know about God's plan of salvation . . . , a perfect participation in God's life through the Son in the Holy Spirit, we may assume with some probability the same supernatural goal for all other possible spiritual beings."[10] Religious phrases about "covenant" or "redemption" do not exhaust the ways by which divine power can share its life of love and mercy. So there might be a variety of ways by which God gives information and love to intelligent creatures on a thousand planets. Those modes of revelation and graced life could differ from galaxy to galaxy.

9. Some theological traditions like the Franciscan school or churches in Eastern Orthodoxy hold that intelligence calls forth from a freely generous God some sharing in divine life. Other, largely Western, theologies can imagine them living in a purely natural world, living without grace.

10. Roch Kereszty, "Christ and Possible Other Universes and Extraterrestrial Intelligent Beings," in *Jesus Christ: Fundamentals of Christology* (New York: Alba House, 1991), 380.

There are millions of bands on the spectrum of natural life on Earth. Is it not likely that there are multiple forms of supernatural life? In a billion solar systems, the forms of love, created and uncreated, would not be limited. Realizations of divine life would not be in contradiction with each other or with creation. On Earth, Buddhists and Jews, Hindus and Coptic Christians have different understandings of the graced person. How would quite different creatures understand God's nearness and transcendence? In distant solar systems and civilizations, surprising articulations of love and growth might flourish.

Forms of Evil and Sin

As there might be multiple kinds of extraterrestrial persons and modalities of divine presence, so evil can assume distinct forms. There are physical evils like illness and death, floods and storms. There is also freely committed human violence toward self and others—actions called sins. The free, destructive choices called sins are personal, moral realizations of evil. Not only do individual acts injure people on Earth—on our planet there seems to be an atmosphere, a dynamic, of evil. It renders bad decisions, crime, and corruption too easy and too frequent. Daily life teaches that evil can be a collective as well as an individual contagion; a past fall never ceases to be active in the personalities of all men and women.

There is no reason to think that evil exists anywhere necessarily. The cosmos and revelation both teach that loving wisdom does not create beings evil by nature. Life, love, hope, energy—activities anticipated in animals and realized in persons—are good. Terrestrial intersections of natural forces like geological and atmospheric conditions produce seismic quakes and hurricanes. Elsewhere, however, planets circling their suns might be formed without implanting such disruptive forces. There might be planets where natural destruction is not needed for evolution.[11]

11. See the essays in Ted Peters et al., *The Evolution of Evil* (Göttingen: Vandenhoeck & Ruprecht, 2008).

Modern philosophers, devout believers, scientists, and artists not infrequently see evil as the necessary result of someone having intelligence and freedom. In that approach, choices for violence toward others result directly just from being intelligent and free. For Origen, metaphysical and physical separation from the Supreme Intelligence brought about moral corruption; for Friedrich Schelling, there was an inevitable moral fall when beings fell into limitation from the Godhead as God sought to become itself; and for Paul Tillich, existence alone involves selfishness. Modern theater and modern fiction are often tragic, as they explore the inner depths of people at the edge of violence or hopelessness. Philosophers in the twentieth century, a time marked by horror, see moral failure as an intrinsic concomitant of freedom. Thomas Mann wrote, "It has been said that there would be no philosophy without evil."[12]

Why this presumption of evil? A presumption of universal evil is found regularly in the popular and in the scientific imagination (the next chapter points out the preference of science fiction for "aliens" to be violent). One source for the projection of evil is the fear of others—of "aliens." Second, America has been and is home to religious sects all too ready to depict in frightening images groups outside their own dogma and church. Third, in not a few writings contemporary scientists equate intelligence with evil; they assert pessimistically that the efforts to communicate with other worlds will meet only silence because technologically advanced societies would have destroyed themselves. Some scientists have espoused an almost religious view of widespread evil. Curiously, it seems that here secularism and modern science and agnosticism, supposed liberations from religion, support at times a fundamentalist religiosity of evil. Behind this is the presumption that to have freedom is to use it badly, to live in society is to live in a society of the greedy and violent, and to exist is to threaten and to be threatened. Intelligent civilizations would have their own histories and their own histories of good and evil. Sin in those races might not weaken the personality extensively (as on Earth); sin might touch individuals but not the collectivity (as Earth's transmission of original sin does). Earth should not project a fallen condition, a proneness to all kinds of

---

12. *Thomas Mann Brevier* (Stuttgart: Reclam, 1994), 102.

violence upon other planets. Nonetheless, when evil exists, it could have its own modalities, and there need not be a dull sameness about evil present in persons. It might be that in the universe beings with free choice avoid moral evil and that few civilizations experience sin. In the cosmos of the novels of science fiction by C. S. Lewis, evil is rare. Planets hold peoples who are benign and wise. There is one exception, the isolated "silent planet": Earth.[13]

Star-Friends

This initial analysis of other kinds of intelligent creatures according to a basic religious triad raises the possibility of a variety of forms of freedom responding to God's personal contact. And too, in terms of that triad, human beings should not project terrestrial religion onto possible peoples elsewhere.

If there are many planets and some are destined to be the environment for intelligent civilizations, might not forms of intelligent life eventually be teachers and colleagues for human beings? They may teach others science and technology; they might also be theologians. Is this or that planet a school, a place of learning and maturing for peoples from other planets?

Thinking about extraterrestrials can open scientists and artists and theologians on Earth to wider horizons. Clusters of galaxies may be populated by creatures who in culture and grace are our relatives, our friends. The role of Christianity is not to point to itself at the expense of others but to announce a history on Earth of God's love. God's wise love is powerful; its goal is global. We should look without fear for our cousins in space. It may be that we are related to other planets not only by intelligence and science but also by art and music. The community of galaxies would be one of gifted intelligence and varied presences of God.

13. C. S. Lewis, *Out of the Silent Planet* (New York: Macmillan, 1990), 130. Voltaire agreed: "In the hundred thousand millions of worlds dispersed over the regions of space everything goes on by degrees. . . . Our little terraqueous globe here is the madhouse of those hundred thousand millions of worlds. . . ." "Memnon," in *Favorite Works of Voltaire* (Garden City, NY: De Luxe, 1900), 265.

chapter three

From a Violent Planet to the Universe of a Loving God

I f there are extraterrestrials, what would they be like? What would be their religious perspective? How to imagine the variety with which ten or a thousand civilizations depict and worship God? An infinite being would relate in many ways to all these intelligences in their ages and galaxies and with their own gifts.

Philosophy, theology, and art have spoken of God—not infrequently with reservations, because mature thinkers conclude that God is not easily or fully knowable. God is in fact not much like beings in the universe: God is not one great being and is not the collectivity of all beings. The complex and still ungrasped dynamics of the galaxies is a reminder that a very different reality lies at their beginnings. To appreciate the extent of the universe is to appreciate how the source differs from all that it has summoned forth by the gift of existence. Galactic reflections lead away from immature theologies.

A Generous Artist

The size and complexity of the universe suggest that the concert of galaxies is not self-referential but points to a fashioning power. Can there be anything or anyone who isn't much like what we see on Earth? Can there be an eternal One who fashions time, an endless creativity behind so many species? The universe intimates intelligence and power, variety and vitality.

Black holes, dimensions beyond the ordinary three dimensions, parallel universes, antimatter—these suggest mystery and depth. Christian mystics and philosophical theologians posit a divine life at the edge of reality. The Creator reveals itself in the universe of beings and then further in modes of revelation and inspiration. Creation and divine love of creatures originate in the unknown depths of the Godhead and move out into space and time to express God's external life. God is not lonely, not a solitary being waiting for the appearance of a few beings to bring companions. God is not an engine, a judge, or an experimenting technician; nor is God a potentiality awakening to action in an eternal night. God is not part of the physical universe of gas and fire, not a past hard-working cause that has since gone missing because it is no longer needed. God is not the repairperson of a machine nor the fixer of gaps in creation or history. Further, God is not the religious patron of bellicose peoples and not the spark of miracles and prodigies in the clouds; nor is God mainly a king of angels and disembodied souls. Hans Küng ponders the differences of created and uncreated light: "The nature of light is constantly being further explored, and perhaps one day it will be possible to explain the mystery of light. But the mystery of God remains: God remains the infinite, immeasurable, unfathomable, and unites in himself opposites such as eternity and temporality, distance and nearness, justice and mercy, anger and grace. He is as hidden in the cosmos as in my heart, decidedly more than a person and yet capable of being addressed at any time."[1]

A theological consideration of the universe begins not with the mechanics of causes but with the wisdom of plans. Astronomical sciences research the laws, patterns, and dynamics beneath the phenomena of stars and find new and amazing arrangements. There is little evidence of randomness or chance. Order within order and diversity within plurality suggest not a machine but an artist. God is related to the universe in many ways: as cause, as planner, as lover. Thomas Aquinas in the thirteenth century, inspired by both natural science

1. Hans Küng, *The Beginning of All Things: Science and Religion* (Grand Rapids: Eerdmans, 2009), 126.

and the Bible, wrote of nature as a gift, as "the art of divine wisdom and the realm of divine goodness."[2] Out of the ideas of all things that could exist, God artistically creates the cosmos.[3] It belongs to wisdom to have all-encompassing plans, and those plans await the research of intelligences around the universe. God intends a universe that is diverse and—through variety—precisely and coherently arranged. God, needing nothing, is drawn by goodness to bestow existence on others. God's generosity comes from goodness without limit and realizes itself in giving. Because generous wisdom cannot be represented by only a few creatures, he has created a huge variety: particles, chemicals, plants, and animals, all in millions of kinds.

Both God and the human race have dimensions of transcendence and immanence; both live in the tension between creation and evolution.[4] Higher fields of activity include the existence and activity of lower levels of action. Galactic modes of development after creation glorify God in their diversity and independence. The potentiality to evolve, to unfold in myriads of forms, indicates not chaos but original power. God can call into existence and direct at levels that are difficult for us to imagine. All this points to a being that is not like created agents. Roch Kereszty writes, "In a theological sense all possible universes would converge in an ultimate unity, because there is only one God, the alpha and the omega of all created worlds. . . . [People on Earth] would not face any being that would be completely 'alien,' or completely different from them. All universes would find a common home in God, and through God man would find an extended home in all the universes."[5] Who is this superbeing who knows and foresees the dynamics of all the elements and animals in all the galaxies? Could the Ultimate touch every person on every

2. Aquinas, *Summa Theologiae* III, 1, 1, 3.

3. Ibid. I, 14, 8. "The power of God—that is his very essence and also his wisdom." Ibid. I, 25, 5. See further sections on Thomas Aquinas' theology in chapter seven.

4. See the essays in Ted Peters, ed., *Cosmos as Creation: Theology and Science in Consonance* (Nashville: Abingdon, 1989), and those in Clifford N. Matthews and Roy Abraham Varghese, eds., *Cosmic Beginnings and Human Ends: Where Science and Religion Meet* (Chicago: Open Court, 1995).

5. Roch Kereszty, "Appendix II," in *Jesus Christ: Fundamentals of Christology* (New York: Alba House, 1991), 378.

planet in every galaxy? God is immanent to the world and at the same time distinct from it. Somehow a boundlessness encompasses finite structures and processes. Joseph Bracken explains: "The world of creation originally came into being and still continues to exist within this divine field of activity. Since the divine field of activity is infinite or strictly unlimited, creation cannot exist apart from God but only in God. Yet since creation as a whole is to be understood as a complex set of overlapping and hierarchically ordered fields of activity for created actual occasions, it can exist within the divine field of activity and yet retain its own ontological identity apart from the three divine persons."[6] Having drawn realities into existence billions of years ago, God will continue to be active in the birth of stars millennia from now. How is God present in the lives of intelligent creatures yet to emerge? As a force or as a friend? Eminent freedom enables wise plans to become concrete. Perhaps today on another world, animals have reached intelligence.

God as the creator of beings-in-process is the creator of time. God is not subject to temporality, and yet he is not alien to it. Aquinas wrote, "Even before contingent beings come into existence God sees them as they actually exist, and not merely as they will be in the future or as they are present in their causes. His eternity is his contact in a present moment with the whole course of time."[7] God is free because he knows in an intimate but sovereign way the totality of the universe and the movements of each star cluster in it:

> The divine persons existing within the all-encompassing divine field of activity experience what is going on within the world of creation and are able to respond to events taking place within creation more accurately and completely than the mind or soul within a human being is able to monitor what is happening in one's own body and respond to it with one's own decisions. What is key, of course, is that the space/time structure proper to the world as a whole and its various subdivisions is thus in God rather than that

6. Joseph Bracken, "Time and Eternity in Religion and Science," in *Subjectivity, Objectivity and Intersubjectivity: A New Paradigm for Religion and Science* (West Conshohocken, PA: Templeton Foundation Press, 2009), 172.

7. Aquinas, *Opuscula theologica* (Turin: Marietti, 1953), 133.

God is somehow constrained by the space-time parameters of this world in dealing with creation.[8]

Christian theologians hold that the overarching goal of the universe is not to generate countless but similar fiery suns but to fashion beings of awareness and activity, to let persons of creativity and love step forth. The multiple levels of living things on Earth suggest a movement upward. Does not evolution place an emphasis upon higher forms of life? If so, it is likely that the universe contains a considerable variety of life-forms and intelligent species. Their intelligence and freedom invites an intimacy and immortality with God, and so religion and revelation would not be about logical contradictions between cause and effect, infinity and individuality, or eternity and time. Grace in extraterrestrial lives and cultures would be richer than kinds of gravity in clusters of stars. Karl Rahner concludes, "This God is not merely the eternally distant mystery beyond the world and our existence. Rather, this God has made himself the innermost principle of the world's activity. This innermost, divine, fundamental dynamic is at work everywhere in the world and everywhere in history, and in the history of religion too."[9] God is most distant and most near. How will that dialectic play out in billions of gifted minds and wills?

Goodness of Existence or Presumption of Evil?

Modernity does not lack for neuroses. For many, anxiety pervades life and calls for faith or therapy. As if there is not enough conflict on Earth, human entertainment seeks out violence in worlds far away. Does a proneness to evil inevitably flow from intelligence? Will freedom usually choose immorality? Does the self-direction of men and women fall hopelessly into violence? On the other hand, do not the power and beauty of the galaxies point to a quite differ-

8. Bracken, *Subjectivity, Objectivity and Intersubjectivity*, 174f.

9. Rahner, "Christianity's Absolute Claim," *Theological Investigations* 21 (New York: Crossroad, 1988), 175. Here we must recall Aquinas' opinion that a single free, intelligent creature touched by God's grace is more valuable than the entire material universe (*Summa Theologiae* I-II, 113, 9, 2).

ent framework of reality where variety and unfolding order are the gifts of generosity?

Movies, novels, and television offer vivid descriptions of creatures arriving from other planets in rather primitive space ships; they have the forms of a huge animal or of a bacterium. For centuries, writers have fashioned plots centering on beings from outer space. Jules Verne, the pulp magazines of the 1940s, and the B movies of the 1950s have left behind a legacy of the exciting and the bizarre. For H. G. Wells, a militant atheist, the world of the future would have utterly replaced religion with technology. Space heroes in Hollywood movies were much the same as Superman. In the 1980s with *ET*, *Close Encounters of the Third Kind*, and *Cocoon*, extraterrestrials were benign. Since the 1990s, they have become, more often than not, violent. Theology need not spend much time on these images, for they are entertainment.[10]

Not much science fiction alludes to religion. Among terrestrial civilizations it is hard to find one that does not have some religious orientation and context. Why would this not be true in other galaxies? Often there are imitations of Roman religion or medieval liturgy, but mature faith and revelation are absent in the novels. If at times there is a religious coloring to the gatherings of extraterrestrials, there are no clear religious ideas, no wisdom or hope. A few writers have offered a religious view. C. S. Lewis explored original sin and original grace on other planets. The temptation of an intelligent

10. See Andrew Fraknoi, *Science Fiction Stories with Good Astronomy and Physics: A Topical Index*, Astronomical Society of the Pacific website (http://astrosociety.org/education/resources/scifiprint.html); Susan Schneider, ed., *Science Fiction and Philosophy: From Time Travel to Superintelligence* (Malden, MA: Wiley-Blackwell, 2009); Thomas M. Disch, *The Dreams Our Stuff Is Made Of* (New York: The Free Press, 1998); Douglas R. Cowan, *Sacred Space: The Quest for Transcendence in Science Fiction, Film, and Television* (Waco, TX: Baylor University Press, 2010); Thomas P. Weber, ed., *Science and Fiction: Leben auf anderen Sternen*, 2 vols. (Frankfurt: Fischer, 2004); David Darling, "Science Fiction," in *The Extraterrestrial Encyclopedia* (New York: Three Rivers, 2000), 370–72; Charles P. Mitch, *A Guide to Apocalyptic Cinema* (Westport: Greenwood Press, 2001); Mayo Mohs, "Introduction" in *Other Worlds, Other Gods: Adventures in Religious Science Fiction* (Garden City: Doubleday, 1971), 10–18; Kingsley Amis, *New Maps of Hell* (New York: Harcourt Brace and Co., 1960).

race, the aggression of satanic forces, and the struggle of good and evil in other Adams and Eves takes place. His universe, however, is a society of planets holding civilizations and peoples who are wise and loving. Sin is a rarity.[11] Arthur C. Clarke pursued a different perspective, one where persons passed into atmospheres of evil. In his *Against the Fall of Night*, superbeings were created by an artificial human religion. When novels and short stories in past decades treat religion, they often depict more intense modes of Earth's religions: the total absence of sin, a Buddhist wisdom, a Christian activism. Jesus or a Christ figure may appear as a variant on the Jesus of the New Testament. However, what incarnation means and what it means for people is avoided; liturgies, sacramental and cosmic, are likewise absent.

Science fiction films and books are by and large not imaginatively drawn. Would extraterrestrial intelligences resemble people or plants on Earth? Why would having a large head or an extra eye be a sign of living in a distant galaxy? The spacecrafts racing across screens in theaters are large and cumbersome versions of airplanes imagined years ago. On television a tour of planets and solar systems is not much different from flying around Earth. Intelligent and communicative life-forms from other planets appear grotesque and threatening, and their intensions are usually hostile. Earthlings learn immediately that aliens are intent on destroying all they encounter; extraterrestrials, whether terrorizing innocent vacationers or challenging the president of the United States, bring vast destruction—even the end of terrestrial civilization. We learn nothing about their worlds of art and mysticism, their sociology and technology. (One thing we do learn repeatedly and clearly: ETs hate New York City.) Some recent criticism of science fiction, however, looks at the most recent films and television in light of the human quest for self-transcendence and modes of divine presence; it observes that religious forms are now more related to recent technological sophistication and have set aside the emphasis on horror.

Inspiration for scenarios of violence and destruction can come from sectarian and apocalyptic religion so prominent in American

11. S. Schwarz, *C. S. Lewis on the Final Frontier: Science and the Supernatural* (Oxford: Oxford University Press, 2009).

history. Moreover, some contemporary scientists equate intelligence with evil and join technology with bellicosity.[12] They conclude that efforts to communicate with other worlds will meet silence because technologically advanced societies inevitably would have destroyed themselves. Certainly violence and technology in the hands of the egotistical will not assist exploration. Tranquility and stability are a prerequisite for a society willing to make the expensive and prolonged effort required to contact another world. Other scientists expect a positive evolution in civilizations whose technology could contact us. A further theory is that extraterrestrials do have the ability and the will to contact Earth, but in the interest of not harming our culture by revealing themselves prematurely, they hold back; they are refraining from contact until the human race is mature enough to handle the experience.

The universe has a beauty bestowed through aesthetic forms; laws and phenomena lead on to realms awaiting research. In theory, if not on Earth, evil would indeed seem to be an exception. Because the universe indicates great variety and intricacy, theologians presume a God of imagination and capability. It would be paradoxical if theologians held an optimistic view of extraterrrestrials on other planets, while scientists and novelists cultivated pessimistic scenarios.

Communities in the Universe

One can read in books and journals that ninety percent of the universe appears to be empty. Science once delighted in discovering absence in space. The void had an ideology associated with it: it was a sign of absence, a statement of a lack of origin and destiny, an indication of no God. The universe was not populated with gods or angels or beings but empty. Great emptiness does exist, but it sets off countless stars that contain a thousand times the mass of the Sun and are born from clouds of gas and dust.

---

12. An intersection of galaxies is involved in "cannibalism," while "violent" explosions of gasses lead to "ferocious stars," "cold wars," "destruction," "no hope of escape," and "bangs." See "The Violent Universe," in *Astronomica*, ed. Fred Watson (Elanora Heights, Australia: Millennium House, 2007), 142–47.

The universe in many ways points to community. Where in the great emptiness there are galaxies and stars, they often exist in groups. As we saw, Earth's galaxy moves in a cluster of six galaxies and then further in a group holding about thirty galaxies. Beyond clusters of galaxies there are what are called "superclusters." "Enmeshed in this cosmic network are individual galaxies, galaxy clusters, and, even more mystifying, agglomerations of galaxy clusters termed 'superclusters.'"[13] They usually contain on average upward of fifty thousand galaxies within a diameter of two hundred million to three hundred million light-years. Superclusters hold forces important for star formation.

Within galaxies there are further clusters—clusters of stars. Stars are not uniformly scattered throughout the universe but also exist in clusters, miniclusters, and superclusters. A cluster may have three hundred to three hundred thousand stars. There are about 150 good-sized clusters in the Milky Way with some still to be discovered. The Andromeda galaxy may have as many as five hundred clusters, while some giant elliptical galaxies have thirteen thousand globular clusters. Clustering draws stars from one cluster to another cluster and even to another region of the galaxy.[14] The stellar dynamic of moving and regrouping offers opportunities to interact and so to stimulate star formation. Where there are stars there are planets. Probably on yet another world, plants and fish and mammals are evolving into higher forms and so preparing for the arrival of intelligence. And so a dynamic of gathering and clustering reaches out extensively to galaxies and stars.

According to Christian faith, the depths of God also reveal a community, a plurality. The Christian God is not a monarch but a trinity. Walter Kasper writes, "Neither the substance of the ancients nor the person of the moderns is ultimate, but rather relation is the primordial category of reality."[15] The universe's structure is re-

13. Bruce Dorminey, "What Galaxy Superclusters Tell Us about the Universe," *Astronomy* (January 2010): 28f.

14. "Star Clusters," in *Astronomica*, ed. Watson, 148–50; see Gary Mechler, *Galaxies and Other Deep-Sky Objects* (New York: Knopf, 1995), 92.

15. Kasper, *The God of Jesus Christ* (New York: Crossroad, 1984), 290. On the history of Christian theology sustaining the theory that creation is attributed to

lated to the communion of intelligence and love. Joseph Bracken develops a metaphysics of universal intersubjectivity as illuminating God and the world. Access to God lies in diversity: in community more than in the single solitary, so beloved of past philosophies and political structures—particularly Western ones. The Trinity is the intradivine reality of God. The universe "can and should be understood dynamically in terms of the unchanging but still continuous relations of the three divine persons to one another even apart from the reality of creation."[16] Gisbert Greshake writes, "Creation is determined through relationality and complementarity, plurality and communality. All these realities are in their simplest form characterized by threefoldness."[17] The divine is giving—self-giving to each divine person and then in time and space self-giving to intelligent creatures. "God is that communion in which three divine persons in a trialogical mutual activity of love realize one divine life through mutual self-sharing."[18] On Earth human persons live in social settings. There is a dialectic of person and group; the metaphor of the "reign of God" expresses a loving society for people is expressed by St. Paul, who spoke of *pleroma*, a "fullness" related to the life of others. The final state of Earth is a communality of billions of men and women in multiple transformations: personal, social, cosmic. Christian revelation's access to the Trinity is much more than a dogma or a puzzle: it is an opening into the structure of reality, divine and created.

The human race on Earth and structures in the stars point to community. Galaxies spend their lengthy times of existence in groups, coming together and modifying each other. Apparently interactivity and community are patterns in reality reaching from the Trinity to

---

the one God and not to any person of the Trinity, see Gisbert Greshake, *Der dreieine Gott: Eine trinitarische Theologie* (Freiburg: Herder, 1997), 32–39.

16. Joseph Bracken, *The One in the Many: A Contemporary Reconstruction of the God-World Relationship* (Grand Rapids: Eerdmans, 2001), 215–17.

17. Greshake, *Der dreieine Gott: Eine trinitarische Theologie*, 248. Contemporary theologians like Greshake and Jürgen Moltmann have drawn trinitarian theology into "the communicality of creation." On a planet or in a galaxy, past dialectics of one and many, identity and difference now yield to communities and networks. Ibid., 248–52.

18. Ibid., 179.

the families of stars. Possibly there lies ahead in Earth's future not only the knowledge of individual planets with their societies but also an awareness of galactic communality. Clusters of planets could share progress in science and art. There would be collective ministries and destinies among the stars and their planets.

Surprising arrangements of matter and spirit, with their own means of interplay and communication, suggest experiences of what the universe has just begun. The divine emerges less through mechanics and authority and more through plan and presence. Surprisingly, the variety of beings, the complex process through stages of life, and even community and society point to new theologies.

chapter four

Jesus of Nazareth and the Galaxies

Will lines of evolution in the universe follow original paths? Complex arrangements of matter may produce suns with planets and moons. They may produce planets like ours or planets with unusual life-forms. Some planets with extraterrestrial civilizations may be twins, cousins, or colonies of other planets.

Religion on Earth, proclaimed and celebrated by human beings, usually affirms God acting in human life. The Spirit of God is at work in the billions of terrestrial men and women, moving within their religious quests. A believer holds that revelation and personal assistance from God to people can find expression in language, architecture, and ritual. Christians believe that human religious quest and divine revelation meet in the teaching of Jesus. His life, death, and resurrection confirm his teaching about a richer life of love on Earth and a future life after death. It is the climax of the Christian narrative of salvation in history.

Human intelligence is transcendence in matter. God has decided to give himself in more profound ways to the creatures that seek life and transcendence. God in an ecstasy of love gives to Earth a profound but concrete form: the divine becomes a human being to prove love.[1] Christians believe that Jesus is the intense realization, the incarnation, of a special presence called "revelation" or "grace."

---

1. See Rahner, "Christology in the Setting of Modern Man's Understanding of Himself and of His World," *Theological Investigations* 9 (New York: Seabury,

The Word of God as a Person on Earth: Jesus of Nazareth

Faith affirms that the divine reality—named by Christians as "Word" or "Son"—has become incarnate, has become a human being on planet Earth. For St. Paul, Jesus is an image of God and a prototype of the human race: "He is the image of the invisible God, the first-born of all creation" (Col 1:15). For Thomas Aquinas, incarnation is a manifestation, visible and intense, of the divine in the human. On Earth the divine agent is not quite the deity itself but one of the persons of the Trinity. Incarnation is interpersonal. Love cannot be more present than in the action of becoming one human being on one planet. An incarnation is not God replacing the human brain or limbs. Through centuries of reflection believers have come to see incarnation as a special divine presence and activity flowing into the totality of one human being. Early Christianity, its opponents and its defenders, understood well that the newness and shock of its message of incarnation was not that God was on Earth (the theme of many religious myths) but that God had become a human being. What is the minimum for incarnation? Intelligence and freedom, individuality and personality receive the divine person. In Jesus three realities meet: human nature, divine nature, and divine person.

The opposite of religious isolation is incarnation. Jesus' teaching describes God's love in a realm, a "kingdom," of peace and love and service. He does not bring magic and conundrums but shows concretely a little of what God is like in terms of human life. The Word of God in Jesus has a particular relationship to terrestrials according to the religious triad we saw above—person, grace, and sin. Jesus the teacher is also a cause of eternal life and of grace countering sin. His resurrection displays a physical life in a different kind of time, space, and matter. References to Jesus' being above the heavens and above angelic mediators are not astronomical facts but rhetorical emphases of his special relationship to people on Earth.

1974), 218f. Viewing Jesus himself as an extraterrestrial is David Wilkinson, "Was Jesus a Space Alien?" in *Alone in the Universe* (Downers Grove, IL: InterVarsity Press, 1997), 100–114.

The astronomy of the Hellenistic period studied the planets and a sphere of fixed stars. Religious sects devoted to angels and sponsoring shrines to appease powerful forces through sacral rites did not in those times know the structure and breadth of the universe as they are understood in the twenty-first century. The New Testament is reticent about any world beyond Earth. Texts emphasizing Jesus' centrality were not composed by writers who imagined peoples on planets. Jesus alluded to angels and evil spirits, while St. Paul mentioned different kinds of lofty created beings called in his times by names like "powers" and "principalities." More or less spiritual or corporeal, more or less aesthetic or mythical, these are agents and objects of the religions of the time. Christians, however, confessed that the central plan of love and life comes not from dramatic spirits but from God through Jesus. Men and women individually loved by God need not appease or fear nonexistent beings. At no point in Christian Scriptures do we learn that there is another race of knowing corporeal beings in the universe—or that there is not.

Christians describe Jesus as Son of God, Word of God, Redeemer, and Savior. Each designation is an English expression of what originally was Hebrew, Latin, or Greek. Each term has a long history, each is limited, and each joins a complex human reality together with a mysterious divine one. Christians can sum up too succinctly the reality of Jesus. Largely expressed in what was originally Greek metaphysics, dogmatic definitions try to encapsulate a reality; inevitably their truth is limited and seminal. Statements about Jesus are sometimes popular, devotional expressions; they can bring exaggerations. The man Jesus is not eternal without qualifications: he is not a magician; he is not a human container of divine power.

Incarnation has a positive, anthropocentric focus: Jesus is the center of God's presence for the human race on Earth. Jesus teaches the plan of God for Earth. Apparently the gift of God's friendship and forgiveness has an intrinsic movement toward the concrete and the personal, toward becoming the one loved. The drive of the human person toward that which is greater and the development of the cosmos tend toward an incarnational dynamic. There is a multiplicity of God's presence in the cosmos. The self-transcendence of the material universe finds particularity in the aspirations of the human person, while in human history God's grace moves toward deeper fulfillment. This happens in all men and women, although it happens in a unique way in incarnation. God in silence and mystery unfolds over vast stretches of time new ways of bringing existence and life. Will not evolution toward consciousness, toward maturity, invite incarnation in other planetary civilizations? The "economy of salvation," a central phrase of Greek Christian theologians, could be wider than one divine plan for Earth. Incarnation is not a phenomenon utterly separate from the cosmos but a sign of its dignity and future. Placing Jesus in a cosmic context gives a deeper understanding of his person and his teaching.[2]

Jesus of Nazareth and the Cosmos

God's relationships with creatures have at times a personal tonality. In Jesus the Word of God becomes fully a particular human being with physical, psychological, and social forms. Christian reflection on the incarnation long expressed itself mainly in metaphysical and legal terms. Recent theologies, however, emphasize Jesus the Christ as a human individual. They explore the religious and political worlds in which he moved and look at his development, his companions, his followers, and his enemies.[3]

Christology, the theology of the Christ, would face two questions as it enters a wider cosmos. Is Jesus of Nazareth on Earth utterly unique in the universe? Are there passages in the New Testament giving Jesus of Nazareth temporal and cosmic relationships to other

2. With the phrase "hypostatic union" Christian Greek theologies mean that one coordinating divine person takes on a fully individualized human nature. The Word sustains metaphysically the man Jesus. Exotheologies with a wider perspective would have to be wary of the possible intrusions of contemporary forms of the old christological errors like Monophysitism, Arianism, and Docetism. Pierre Teilhard de Chardin spoke of the need for a further Council of Nicaea to face the issues of the historical Jesus and the cosmic Jesus Christ. See J. A. Lyons, *The Cosmic Christ in Origen and Teilhard de Chardin* (London: Oxford University Press, 1982), 41.

3. See Ilia Delio, *Christ in Evolution* (Maryknoll, NY: Orbis, 2008); Juan Luis Segundo, *An Evolutionary Approach to Jesus of Nazareth* (Maryknoll, NY: Orbis, 1988).

planets? There are lines in the early Christian *Letter to the Colossians* linking Jesus Christ to the universe. "He is the image of the invisible God, the first-born of all creation; for in him all things were created, in heaven and on earth, visible and invisible, whether thrones or dominions or principalities or authorities—all things were created through him and for him. He is before all things, and in him all things hold together. He is the head of the body, the church; he is the beginning, the first-born from the dead, that in everything he might be preeminent" (Col 1:15-18). Exegetes see these words as a hymn of the early church. Who is the "he" of this passage? The historical Jesus did not exist prior to creation, for he was born around 4 BCE. The subject of these lines is the divine being called Word or Son. The Word's incarnational mode, Jesus, son of Joseph, was not historically present at creation.

Jewish speculation about a divine Wisdom is present in those lines about the preexistent Christ as holder of the plan for the cosmos. The Word of God as Wisdom implies rational and beautiful orderings; creative power and love also render Wisdom leader and exemplar.[4] As Wisdom in the form of a human being, Jesus Christ is superior over all mythical religious forces. No angels or cosmic powers, no stars or planets are bearers of God's revelation for Earth in any way comparable to him.[5] The text is concerned not with an eternal semidivine being but with the superiority of Jesus because he is an agent of eternal plans.[6]

---

4. Eduard Lohse, *Colossians and Philemon* (Philadelphia: Fortress, 1971), 50. See also Raymond Brown, "Incarnate Wisdom," in *An Introduction to New Testament Christology* (Mahwah: Paulist Press, 1994), 205–11; M. E. Willett, *Wisdom Christology in the Fourth Gospel* (San Francisco: Mellen, 1992).

5. Cf. Col 1:16; 2:20; see Jean-Noël Aletti, *Saint Paul: Épitre aux Colossiens* (Paris: Gabalda, 1993), 117f.; W. Kern, "Die antizipierte Entideologisierung oder die 'Weltelemente' des Galater- und Kolosserbriefes heute," *Zeitschrift für katholische Theologie* 96 (1974): 185–216.

6. Lohse, *Colossians and Philemon*, 49. Hans Hübner also understands the subject of the "first-born of all creation" to be a preexistent Christ related to Wisdom in the Hebrew Scriptures. The point of the passage is that in terms of personalities in cosmic religion there are no rivals to Jesus. Hübner, *An Philemon, An die Kolosser, An die Epheser* (Tübingen: Mohr, 1997), 59.

For some scholars, the church and not the cosmos is the central topic here. A subsequent verse referring to church and resurrection is the key: "He is the head of the body, the church; he is the beginning, the first-born from the dead" (Col 1:18). The focal point lies in the future rather than in the past. Christ is the firstborn of a new creation, a creation of love, meaning, and eternal life. Creation here means not stars but life in Christ's body, the church. André Feuillet writes, "The Pauline perspective [is] much more religious than cosmological. . . . The uncreated Christ is like a mirror in which God has contemplated the plan of the universe as he creates it. It is in this sense that all has been created in him."[7] Jesus' kingdom of God is a future world, a realm of God restoring human morality and immortality. Jerome Murphy-O'Connor also offers an interpretation shifting from the cosmological to the incarnational and ecclesiological. He too thinks that the opening verses of Colossians about Christ and creation come from an earlier hymn where Paul was criticizing a theology that was too much a cosmology and angelology. It is not a celestial Christ but a Jesus risen to new life that holds sway. "He directs the reader's attention to the physical existence of him who is now the Risen Lord."[8] Far from pursuing cosmology, the subsequent verses introduce the church. "Paul's insistence that Christ is present in him[9] and in all members of the Church draws the cosmic dimension of the Christological reflections of Colossians down into ecclesiology."[10] This theology is not about a Jesus superimposed against the spheres of stars or in company with the demigods of religions but about "the power of God and the wisdom of God" (1 Cor 1:24)[11] at work in salvation history on Earth. The incarna-

---

7. André Feuillet, "La Création de l'Univers 'dans le Christ' d'après l'épître aux Colossiens [I:16a]," *New Testament Studies* 12 (1965–66): 7. See Franz Zeilinger, *Der Erstgeborene der Schöpfung: Untersuchungen zur Formalstruktur und Theologie des Kolosserbriefes* (Vienna: Herder, 1974), 18.

8. Jerome Murphy-O'Connor, "Tradition and Redaction in Col 1:15-20," *Revue Biblique* 102 (1995): 237.

9. Cf. Gal 2:20.

10. Murphy-O'Connor, "Tradition and Redaction," 241.

11. George H. van Kooten concludes that letters speaking of Christ and the cosmos seek to express a wider reality for Jesus as incarnate, for Jesus' humanity. "Christ's cosmic rule, as the author of *Ephesians* makes plain, does not yet

tion is an activity of God moving outward from the Godhead into the world; it is part of a plan that begins with eternal wisdom and ends in history. The cosmos will be increasingly filled with Christ, but that implementation moves through countless men and women and has a dynamic source in the church.

The role of Christ proceeds from incarnation, passes through history and histories, and ends in a transformed cosmos. The risen Christ does have a unique role for Earth. That role has implications for the entire material universe.

Other Incarnations?

Subsequent chapters of this book show that a few ancient and medieval Christian theologians touched briefly on the possibility of an incarnation of God in a creature other than Jesus of Nazareth. All three persons can become incarnate because incarnation is one aspect of boundless divine power. The life of the man Jesus does not curtail the divine Word's being. Could not God become incarnate as God wished? The divine motive for fashioning a universe of galaxies is God's goodness; the same motive brings incarnation. As incarnation is an intense form of divine love, would there not be galactic forms of that love? An infinite being of generosity would tend to many incarnations rather than to one. The inner life of the divine self surging out of three divine persons suggests multiple incarnations; reflection on the dynamics of Trinity and incarnation leads to community and activity and not to isolation. A succession of incarnations would give new relationships and new self-realizations to God. Aquinas offered an insight into God and universe: "The right way to manifest the unseen things of God is through things that are seen, and this is the purpose of the whole world."[12] Incarnations among extraterrestrials would not be competing with us or with each other. The medieval

---

extend over the entire physical cosmos. It began to be implemented when Christ was resurrected and installed in heaven. The benefit of this rule, however, is still limited to the church because Christ has only been given as cosmic head to the church." Van Kooten, *Cosmic Christology in Paul and the Pauline School* (Tübingen: Mohr Siebeck, 2003), 157.

12. Aquinas, *Summa Theologiae* III, 1, *sed contra*.

theologian wrote, "It is appropriate for the highest good to communicate itself to the creature in the highest possible way. . . . Clearly, it was right for God to become incarnate."[13]

Through the centuries Jesus has appeared to some Christians to be identical with the Word of God or to be a body containing God—both views are minimalist. The matter of incarnation is not a shell, a body, or a physical container but the totality of a knowing and free creature that is material and animal. The man Jesus of Nazareth remains minute compared to the Word of God; the reality of a divine person is always open to further realization. Aquinas made a marginal observation in his theology concerning the incarnation of the Word in Jesus Christ that is pertinent. He asked in the thirteenth century whether a divine person could be incarnate in a further creature— someone other than Jesus of Nazareth—and answered affirmatively. "The power of a divine person is infinite and cannot be limited to anything created."[14] Could there not be other incarnations? Perhaps many of them and at the same time? While the Word and Jesus are one, the life of a Jewish prophet on Earth hardly curtails the divine Word's life. The Word loves the intelligent natures it has created, although to us they might seem strange and somewhat repellant.[15] Incarnation is an intense way to reveal, to communicate with an intelligent animal. It is also a dramatic mode of showing love for and identification with that race. In each incarnation, the divine being communicates something from its divine life—but not very much.

Incarnation in a human being speaks to our race. While the possibility of extraterrestrials in the galaxies leads to possible incarnations and alternate salvation histories, incarnations would correspond to the forms of intelligent creatures with their own religious quests. Jesus of Nazareth, however, is a human being and does not move to other planets. There is no incarnation when a divine presence already

---

13. Ibid. III, 1, 1.

14. Ibid. III, 7, 3. Aquinas cites an authority: "As Augustine replies, 'Christian doctrine does not teach that God was so joined to human flesh as to lose or resign control over the universe as though constricted by a baby.'" Ibid. III, 1, 4.

15. See George L. Murphy, "Cosmology and Christology," *Science and Christian Belief* 6 (1994): 109–11.

having assumed a form in a visible species formally addresses a people on another planet. One intelligent species intimately touched by God might be a divine messenger to another intelligent civilization. This, however, is not God incarnate in that people. If the risen Jesus Christ visited another planet, it would be a celestial disclosure, but it would not be a further incarnation.

Each incarnation has its own identity, even as it is sustained by an infinitely removed divine ground.[16] Culturally and religiously each person lives in and out of his or her cultural society. Incarnation is not a form of miracle but an activity of revelation and teaching. Is not incarnation in some ways ordinary and as such not unique to Earth? The abilities of galactic intelligent societies and God's love toward them do not demean Jesus of Nazareth. The possibility of incarnation for extraterrestrials does not diminish the reality of Jesus Christ. Such a view does not necessarily bring a liberal Protestant or Deist view of Jesus as an ethical teacher or a religious myth. Moreover, the complexity of the universe questions a terrestrial limitation of God's power and love. A believed revelation of God to people on Earth—no matter how illuminating it is—should not imply that we comprehend much of the plans of God or gain the right to say what an infinite being can or cannot do.

Salvation Histories amid Galactic Evolution

The incarnation has often been seen as mainly providing a savior for human sins. Jesus the prophet ends up betrayed and executed by evil groups on Earth. This is not the only or the most meaningful Christian theology. Evil cannot be dominant in a creation of beauty and development. The cross should not dominate the theme and reality of incarnation; life exists for life, not death. The crucifixion of the Incarnate One on Earth is the result of terrestrial religious and political rejections of what is good. Redemptive suffering by a savior is not the necessary or full purpose of an incarnation. It need not be the only or even a frequent motivation for other incarnations. The history of sin and salvation recorded in the two testaments of

16. Aquinas, *Summa Theologiae* III, 8, 3.

the Bible is a particular religious history on one planet and not the single framework or the sole history for all civilizations in the universe. The centrality of Jesus, no matter how important to Earth, does not assert claims about other races on other planets and their religious situation amid grace and sin.

Jesus' teaching and life bring an eschatology for Earth and not an astronomy for the Milky Way. The very divine generosity that led once to an incarnation argues that there might be other incarnations in various species, many creatures touched in one or another special way by a person of the Trinity. If, however, there are other intelligent creatures but no incarnations among them, then the union of the Logos and a terrestrial human would be a strong affirmation of the dignity of corporeal, intelligent life wherever it is found. Each incarnation would spotlight and enhance one planet and, through that, a galaxy. Complementarity would invite civilizations with one or many incarnations to teach each other.[17] The full reality of Jesus of Nazareth and the dynamic infinity of God illumine each other against the background of the galaxies. Raimundo Panikkar writes of the mission of expanding Christology: "It is not a question either of supplanting traditional Christology or of forgetting the tradition from which Christianity was born. What we need to do is to revisit the experience of the mystery of Christ in the light of our times—to recognize the *kairos* of the present, even though our need does not spring from an anxiety to be up-to-date. . . . The greatness of the Christian vision does not take anything away from other intuitions of the ultimate mystery of reality."[18] Anthony Godzieba draws modern

---

17. The liturgical and devotional view of Jesus and Mary as presiding over the universe or over angels is not based on their human nature but upon their contact with the Word. If other intelligent creatures have hypostatic or particularly intimate contacts with God, then a Jewish messiah and his mother would not by virtue of the incarnation on our planet be unique or supreme in the cosmos.

18. Raimundo Panikkar, *Christophany: The Fullness of Man* (Maryknoll, NY: Orbis, 2000), 186f. Wolfgang Vondey looks at the cosmos and the Holy Spirit: "The order *of* the cosmos is at the same time the order *in* the cosmos. The concepts of change, process, movement, and organization emerge from the supposed relational order and symmetry of the cosmos and have been fundamental concepts in today's physical cosmology. Yet a pneumatological approach to the Spirit as movement of and in the cosmos has not been proposed. In a

and postmodern anthropologies into the sphere of Christian incarnation. Human social interaction profits from an incarnational imagination:

> The incarnation thus opens up the materiality of the particular as the arena of this receptivity. It impels us to think otherwise about materiality and the possibilities of the particular, that the finite can indeed mediate the infinite. . . . Both the poetic imagination and embodiment as fundamental Christian *practices* suggested by the incarnation are called to be both *aesthetically and politically transfigurative*—in other words, to enact the possibilities that signal not only the participation in divine life that has been promised as our fulfillment, but that also resist the reduction to thing-like status that would signal the death of the body and the death of hope.[19]

The probability of other planetary incarnations develops such insights further.

Noticing traces of God in the universe and observing the variety of creation draws theology away from the late modern twilight of a psychology of religious forms neglecting realities. Attention to the universe offers alternatives to academic theories swallowing up in mental structures a historical revelation of grace for people. Cosmic Christology is more than mental religious myths; it corresponds to a universal presence of the Spirit.

Alice Meynell, a British poet, wrote a poem in 1913 about incarnation as a cosmic reality in multiple worlds. Her literary theology, though brief, is remarkable. At a cosmic gathering of intelligent creatures, the signs of the constellations with their own times and their

---

pneumatological image of the cosmos, the Spirit can be seen as both mover and moved, subject and object of creation." Vondey, "Science and Pneumatology," *Theological Studies* 70 (2009): 34.

19. A. Godzieba, "Knowing Differently: Incarnation, Imagination, and the Body," *Louvain Studies* 32 (2007): 381.

own eternities stand forth. Different histories of grace and different Gospels are occurring on planets of other solar systems. Although science was then unaware of the enormity of the universe, Meynell saw not a few extraterrestrial civilizations but hundreds of thousands.

> But in the eternities,
> Doubtless we shall compare together, hear
> A million alien Gospels, in what guise
> He trod the Pleiades, the Lyre, the Bear.
> O, be prepared, my soul!
> To read the inconceivable, to scan
> The million forms of God those stars unroll
> When, in our turn, we show to them a Man.[20]

20. "Christ in the Universe," in *The Poems of Alice Meynell* (London: Hollis and Carter, 1947), 63–64. The full poem can be found in Guy Consolmagno, *Intelligent Life in the Universe? Catholic Belief and the Search for Extraterrestrial Intelligent Life* (London: Catholic Truth Society, 2005), 47–49.

chapter five

Time and the Futures of Life

The Great Nebula in Orion is visible to the naked eye on a dark winter night. It is 1,500 light-years away from Earth, and so the light completing its journey this day left the nebula as the Franks were occupying the Roman Empire. In galactic terms it is close to Earth. Under the pressure of great heat, Orion's clouds of gasses and dust are forming stars. In the next million years the new stars being born and maturing there will make the region even brighter. Each galaxy has a number of such star-forming regions. The Hubble telescope allows us to see not only new stars but a mist of gas and forces which might develop into their planetary systems. What will future planets have as life-forms?

Astronomy looks into the reality of the universe. Photographs from telescopes in space show more and more galaxies. Their billions of suns may already have planets that came into existence a hundred million years ago. Books on science have in their titles "exploration," "discovery," "light," or "seeing." Faith too is a way of seeing, seeing the divine and the future even as those realms remain unseen. With extraterrestrial considerations, science and faith seek to be a little free of Earth's pull as each explores further worlds: galaxies or the kingdom of God.

Time

Time and history, development and evolution, birth and death—these move through the universe. Time moves forward; some times hold in their futures the rewards of fulfillment. What is time? Is it the motion of the sun? Is it the earth's movement? Is it the inner pulse of a human cardiovascular system? Is it an existential mood? There is the digital time of chronometers, there are times of cultures and ages, and there is also the right moment for an event—kairotic time. Thinkers and scientists offer not a few theories about time, and artists and novelists have composed meditations on time. Augustine wondered if time were less a solar motion and more an interior pulsing atmosphere that ceaselessly modified us, while for Martin Heidegger time was the illuminating backdrop to life and culture rather than the seconds of a chronometer. The poet Rainer Maria Rilke observed, "Das Wissen ist nur in der Zeit" (Knowing takes place only in time).[1] Time is many things: a calculation of light, an observance of movement, an aspect of rationality, or an atmosphere around each person's life.

Time is a rich theme in astrophysics; there is the time of the solar system and the times of galaxies, the factor of relativity and the speed of light. Galaxies generate their stars over hundreds of millions of years, although in terms of the billions of years of the universe this is not a long time. Thus a span of fifty or a hundred thousand years for the history of an intelligent civilization is not much. Extraterrestrial civilizations could have their own modes of temporality and history, and any realm of temporality influences the possibility of them becoming known to Earth.

In the past the universe was thought of as a static unit: it was Earth at the center that alone changed. An evolving universe, however, suggests a variety of futures. Faith holds that there is a history of God's presence among men and women; the messages of the Bible occur in history. Whatever we call God's special presence on Earth—salvation, revelation, grace—it has a history: its course is a "salvation history." Events happen in the history of salvation at the "right time." Jesus of Nazareth, the definitive religious figure, has his own times: a time to be born, a time to teach about God, a time to

1. Rilke, *Das Stunden-Buch* (Leipzig: Insel, 1936), 9. See also I. F. Arens, ed., *Zeit Denken* (Freiburg: Herder, 2010); Reinhard Koselleck, *Futures Past: On the Semantics of Historical Time* (Cambridge, MA: MIT Press, 1985); Koselleck, *Zeitschichten: Studien zur Historik* (Frankfurt: Suhrkamp, 2003).

be attacked, a time to anticipate the future.[2] Christianity proclaims itself to be a faith and a communal religion living in time. Theologies and liturgies are the result of history; their languages are born of different cultural periods. Cosmology need not argue against a salvation history like that recorded in the Bible, but believers must be prepared for a galactic horizon and pluralism. The future is to be sought not in the last book of the Christian Bible, the book of Revelation, with its violent dramas and transcendent processions enacted by symbolic groups. It is to be found in the first book of the Bible, Genesis. Perhaps a hundred thousand times, God has said as in Genesis, "Let us make man in our image, after our likeness" (Gen 1:26). In these creatures the activity of the Creator and the love of the Trinity may bring intense levels of knowing and discovering.

Contemporary theologians have been looking at a wider world in terms of salvation history. Thomas Berry writes, "Just as Christianity in its developing phase established itself in intimate relations with the structure and functioning of the universe in its liturgical processes, so now there is a need to adopt a new sense of a self-emergent universe as a sacred mode whereby the divine becomes present to the human community . . . [and] to the universe in its comprehensive dimensions, for indeed the universe is the only self-referent mode of being in the phenomenal world. . . . The purpose of the universe is not focused on any one single being but depends on the entire multiplicity of beings."[3] Far from pitting science against religion, human reflection includes both as contributors to what is salutary for people. "Thus revelation, incarnation and redemption are primarily for the entire universe, not primarily for any group of individual beings within the universe."[4] Gideon Goosen interprets trinitarian activity and sacramental displays of grace in matter as themes of "Spacetime."[5] That scientific and religious grasp of the universe, a

2. Cf. Gal 4:4.

3. Thomas Berry, "The Universe as Cosmic Liturgy," in *The Christian Future and the Fate of Earth* (Maryknoll, NY: Orbis, 2009), 115.

4. Ibid., 117.

5. Gideon Goosen, *Spacetime and Theology in Dialogue* (Milwaukee: Marquette University Press, 2008). Alexei Nesteruk develops the themes of science, universe, and community in light of Christian Orthodox and patristic theologies

theology of space and time, is not a text or a dogma but an explora-tion of mystery. In the past the universe had a sacral character; its forces and beings owned a divine touch or voice or power. Christian motifs can loosen up what seems to be the brittle tension of space/time, and the resulting awareness expands theology. God does not live from moment to moment but exists and lives and loves during all times simultaneously. There is past, present, and future in God's silent guidance of the universe with its citizens. The experience of matter, the experience of space, the experience of time—these are always experiences of "the More."

Other Times

As we saw, both space and time make contact with other civiliza-tions difficult. Time sets a distance between two entities: they are not contemporaneous with each other. The majority of intelligent civilizations directed by God may belong to the past or to the present or to the future. For humans on Earth, it is not easy to imagine hundreds of millions of years lying ahead of us. We falsely presume that emerging stars, planets, and civilizations lie in the past or in the present. Cosmic evolution has its own times. Timothy Ferris observes, "Life thrived on Earth for billions of years before land plants appeared and populated the continents. Biological evolution is so inherently unpredictable that even if life originated on a planet identical to Earth at the same time it did here, life on that planet today would almost certainly be very different from terrestrial life."[6] In its past and in its future, Earth may miss the flourishing of other civilizations. A meeting with another civilization would occur at a time or period when the cycles of human existence and their existence coincide. However, it is possible that there would be no time during which the history of Earth and the history of another civilization (or hundreds of civilizations) would intersect. Any intelligent species

---

in *The Universe as Communion: Towards a Neo-Patristic Synthesis of Theology and Science* (New York: T. & T. Clark, 2008).

6. Timothy Ferris, "Worlds Apart," *National Geographic* (December 2009): 93.

that learns how to determine the ages of stars and galaxies will also come to this sobering conclusion about the intersection of times.

Planets have their own future. There could be a history for people who have never known hierarchical and feudal social structures and a future for those who have never imagined reality in a Platonic dialectic of shadow and reality. On some planets, religions and their believers may see reality as timeless and changeless. The motif of journey and the dynamic of evolution may be absent. An extraterrestrial civilization may have no drive to change, no desire for what is reached with difficulty, and no tendency to self-destruction. The human race has more often than not focused on the past, on primal times, on classical ages. Astronomy is changing that perspective so that the future, even the distant future, illumines time and technology.

Christianity nourishes a person in a saving history but also enhances the existential time of the individual's spirituality. A personal spiritual life finds strength from God in existence and in communal history. It is precisely time—or rather, different times in this or that galaxy—that would enable divine presence to embrace many civilizations. How would many histories of personal development and religious revelation in faith speak with each other? There would be many salvation histories.

Human lives, destinies, and religions are not mainly based on the past. The future is time that does not yet exist, and yet the future is real in its own way. The future is powerful and mysterious and unknown. What lies in the future for Earth? Taller people, more electronic gadgets, more volumes of journals left unread? Perhaps there are several futures. As important as the "now" is, is it only on Earth that each moment looks to the future? All that is believed in, hoped for, but not yet known draws minds forward. Limitations will be transcended, death will be replaced by life, and communion will be filled with happiness.

Space, Matter, and the Future

Christian faith challenges science not by proclaiming an otherworldly heaven or an annihilation of the cosmos but by asserting a future marked by transformation. In some way transformation addresses all intelligent beings in the cosmos. For each extraterrestrial civilization, as we saw, personality and grace, salvation and revelation could be different. Is there for every intelligent civilization some form of death? On Earth there is a dialectic of life and death. An end of time and life comes to creatures of matter; it is one of their limitations. Death comes from natural forces, from the decline of energies; it is not primarily the result of sin driving out grace but of entropy. Christians and others believe in a world where birth leads to life and where death yields to another life; death and decay are themselves passages into life and light.

A salvation history of grace and revelation, the incarnation of the Word, and the resurrection are particular events within the universe of matter. Are there modes of transformation for each planet, for every knowing and free creature? Resurrection is the entry into a special future where personal identity remains within matter, as temporal and physical aspects are changed, enhanced.[7] The Gospels emphasize that Jesus, the head of the human race, is risen into life, but into a life of a different sort, one marked with a transcendence over—and yet enjoyment of—space and time and matter. Jesus, the first of billions of human beings on Earth to rise, has not gone to some other galaxy. Jesus has entered as a human being into a way of being spirit in matter. The risen Christ is cause and paradigm of vivifying grace in other persons. Divine power in matter does not bring reincarnation—against which sciences also argue—for each human being has a unique individuality. Nor is it a question of a reinsertion of the core person into a different body and brain. The resurrection is not resuscitation, a restoration of the same corporeal person into the same kind of life to repeat his or her natural cycle. The resurrection of Jesus draws human beings into the future and into a different world. "What eye has not seen, nor ear heard, nor the heart of man conceived, what God has prepared for those who love him" (1 Cor 2:9). God's future offers a more humane society, a more divine humanity; there is more acceptance of self and more mercy toward others enabled by God's silent presence. Violence disappears as community and justice triumph.

7. See Ted Peters, "The Physical Body of Immortality," *Science, Theology, and Ethics* (Burlington: Ashgate, 2003), 293–311; Ted Peters, ed., *Resurrection: Theological and Scientific Assessments* (Grand Rapids, MI: Eerdmans, 2002).

The resurrection has to do with the totality of the human person, with body and spirit, in modes of rebirth and fulfillment.[8] The resurrection of the individual seems to be accompanied by some material transformation of the world. What happens in these processes? In a powerful way the world without losing its identity and nature would be drawn into the power of God to complete what God has begun with creation. The human soul passes through death into the universe and so retains material and cosmic existence. "The soul by surrendering its limited bodily structure in death becomes open toward the universe and, in some way, a co-determining factor of the universe in the latter's character as the ground of the personal life of other spiritual corporeal beings."[9] A cosmology that held that every unit of creation and the totality of the universe were essentially headed toward terminal death and destruction would not be acceptable to Christian faith. "For this world as a totality, the process of fermentation has already commenced. Earth is already filled with the forces of this indescribable transformation. Its dynamic is called the *Pneuma* of God."[10] If the resurrection of men and women includes a changed cosmic environment, according to St. Paul, how elements and fiery gasses will alter their natures is left unclear.

Christian faith holds that Earth is drawn toward the future and that the future is moving toward us. The Greek word "eschatology" means the future of ultimate conditions from a religious perspective. Eschatology refers to dramatic changes for happiness and fulfillment. Nevertheless, one can conclude that images and prophecies about

8. See Karl Rahner, "The Resurrection of the Body," in *Theological Investigations* 2 (Baltimore: Helicon, 1963), 203–14; Peter C. Phan, *Eternity in Time: A Study of Karl Rahner's Eschatology* (London: Associated University Press, 1988); Denis Edwards, *Breath of Life: A Theology of the Creator Spirit* (Maryknoll, NY: Orbis, 2004).

9. Rahner, *On the Theology of Death* (New York: Herder and Herder, 1961), 23. The teaching about a purgative time and place between death and heaven found in several forms in religions is pertinent here. Some may not be ready for an intense realm of love and life. Another planet could offer the future stage of the psychologically and morally limited person. Another world could educate them, free them, and lead them to levels of knowledge and maturity.

10. Rahner, "Fest der Zukunft der Welt," *Schriften zur Theologie* 7 (Einsiedeln: Benziger, 1971), 180; translation by the author.

the end of the world are in fact expressing not final violence but new luminosity and power. Only with difficulty, however, do people on Earth describe love, happiness, and enjoyment. Evil is more entertaining; imagination races after what is negative. As the Christian believes in the interplay of the power of a transcendent God with the actions of humans in history, so this dynamic increases, occurring in an intensive and triumphant way in a powerful temporality: an "absolute future." The future renewal of peoples' lives is the spiritualization of the modern idea of progress.[11] Earthlings will be free of gravity to explore worlds, communicating with their artists and mathematicians and mystics.

Jesus taught that the love of God and the love of neighbor belong together. A new awareness of ecosystems brings together matter and life with reverence for their sources. Each person and each day are unique. Similarly, astronomy analyzes the light of each star and therein sees its past and future. A planetary civilization would expand our understanding of God. In the past, the Gospel and the church encountered the cultures of Antioch, Lyons, or Tara, and the message of God in liturgy, religion, and spirituality was enhanced. In the future, Earth would learn the value of thinking and believing in the presence of other truths and systems mirroring their particular modes of reality. Since any set of views would see its limitations, measured after other civilizations, there could be no intellectual or theological autocracy. Dialogue would reveal the depth and riches of what would be held in common. A cosmic view would reveal itself as a divine perspective, transforming the ego and the sect. It is not a question simply of other languages or mathematical axioms. The underlying ways of thinking, of seeing the world, of living in society influence everything we imagined or enacted. Thought-forms and life-forms from other civilizations would draw out further theologies and spiritualities from the Christian faith. Music and textures and colors would fashion art, and new perspectives would unfold architecture. Liturgy would have its proper forms of what is heard and seen in worship. Believers would understand their eschatology

11. See Medard Kehl, *Und was kommt nach dem Ende? Von Weltuntergang und Vollendung, Wiedergeburt und Auferstehung* (Freiburg: Herder, 2000), 139–45.

in relationship to extraterrestrials. The journey of a life of faith into the interior mountain range of which the mystics speak would be explained by other contemplative societies. If now we only glimpse the likelihood of civilizations beyond terrestrial history, in the next life men and women will see societies both like and unlike their own.

The many animal species, the numbers of suns and planets do not point to nihilism and darkness but to life and light. The human intellect has a wonderful capability to know: that is, to bring many beings, countless kinds of plants and animals and suns, into itself. In this way the human person—as hopeful believer or as empirical scientist—inhabits the universe. In an "exotheology," a "galactic theology," God is both more distant and more present, active, and mysterious. Faith affirms that we are not alone, not on Earth or elsewhere. Faith follows science's suggestions that on other planets something awaits us terrestrials: star-colleagues, star-mentors, and star-friends.

chapter six

Intelligent Life in the Universe: Perspectives from Christian Thinkers in Past Centuries

This and the next chapter look at past theologians' views on extraterrestrials. For over two millennia religious thinkers and philosophers have had ideas about a wider universe and other races of intelligence. A first group (in this chapter) reaches to the seventeenth century; a second group (in the next chapter) comes mainly out of the past hundred years.

Could theologians of ancient and medieval times imagine intelligent beings beyond Earth? Was not the human person on Earth eminently the center of those cultures? In Greek culture and Christian medieval schools, philosophers and theologians paid attention to the stars and their implications, and some speculated about whether there could be other "worlds."[1] A few considered intellectual creatures

1. See Steven J. Dick, "One World or an Infinity of Worlds? The Greek Tradition" and "Aristotelian Natural Law versus Divine Omnipotence: the Medieval Tradition," in *Plurality of Worlds: The Origins of the Extraterrestrial Life Debate from Democritus to Kant* (Cambridge: Cambridge University Press, 1982), 6–22, 23–44; Jean-Bruno Renard, *Les extraterrestres: Une nouvelle croyance religieuse?* (Paris: Cerf, 1988), 16–34.

on celestial bodies. Some were encouraged rather than dissuaded by Christian revelation, although authorities in church and academia usually had little sympathy for that viewpoint. Christian philosophical theologians from three periods stand out: Origen from the third century, Thomas Aquinas and Guillaume de Vaurouillon from the Middle Ages, and figures from the Renaissance. So, reflecting on extraterrestrials in light of the Christian teaching on creation and incarnation is not new.

Origen (Third Century)

Living in Hellenistic cultural circles and Christian theological schools in the first centuries after the emergence of the Christian faith, a few theologians held theories about a wider inhabited cosmos. Origen (ca. 185–ca. 254) was a student of Greek science and philosophy. He lived in an intellectual center of Hellenistic culture with a great library and university. A polymath, he pioneered textual criticism while mastering the philosophy and science of his time. At the same time, he was a teacher and preacher in the church of Alexandria. The author of numerous biblical commentaries, he composed the first Christian systematic theology. Time and matter, stars and angels were part of the Alexandrian intellectual world, and in his academic career Origen would have discussed them.

Centuries earlier, Greek astronomy and philosophy had entertained the idea of other worlds. In the sixth century BCE the Ionian philosophers Anaximander and Anaximenes of Miletus spoke of a plurality of worlds, while two centuries later Epicurus held that the universe as a whole is without limits in either space or time.[2] The number of worlds is potentially infinite: some would be like ours and others unlike it. In the second century, five decades or so before Origen, Lucian of Samosata wrote a novel[3] about a visit to the moon

---

2. Jean Heidemann, *Life in the Universe* (New York: McGraw Hill, 1992), 12–14. See J. M. Rist, *Epicurus: An Introduction* (Cambridge: Cambridge University Press, 1972); David Sedley, *Creationism and Its Critics in Antiquity* (Berkeley: University of California Press, 2007).

3. *A True Story*, in *Lucian*, vol. 1, trans. A. M. Harmon (Cambridge, MA: Harvard University Press, 1913).

and to Venus with their inhabitants; his novel would seem to be the earliest work of science fiction.

Christianity teaches clearly that the universe has been created by God. Only a real God can create beings where no being previously existed. Christian theologies in the first centuries of the church built upon Jewish convictions and echoed Greek philosophies as they rejected the Gnostic idea of cooperators, eternal or temporal, working under or with God in creation. Nonetheless, the actions of God in the beginning, according to the Hebrew book of Genesis, were not interpreted by all in the same way. St. Justin Martyr and St. Clement of Alexandria, who lived at the end of the second century, seem to have thought that God made the world out of preexistent, primeval matter. While theologians affirmed the absence of being and time before creation, they knew of scientists who held hypotheses in which time and creation could be cyclical or eternal.

The belief in creation ex nihilo, from nothing, was firmly established at the time of Origen.[4] A vast number of minds were initially created by God to enjoy happiness with him. The Creator first produced free intelligences and then, in a distinctly second stage, matter and nonrational creatures. Wisdom and activity, in eternity and in time, are central to this theology. All the rational creatures—later they became angels, devils, stars, and humans—were created together and as equals. They—Origen calls them "intelligences" rather than "souls"—were absorbed in the contemplation of God. Their attention wandered; they partly lost interest in celestial life, and through that declining contemplation and love, they fell away from their pristine state. They fell in different degrees, and the degree of fall gave diversity to angels and demons in modes of existence, and it diversified human beings in their sensual animality. The preexistent intelligence destined to serve as the soul of Jesus born in Bethlehem did not fall. Joined to the Word of God, this intelligence animated the man Jesus, through whom the Word on Earth explained how to comprehend what has happened, how to live above sensual ma-

4. Origen, *On First Principles* 1.3 (New York: Harper and Row, 1966), 31; Hans Jonas, "Origen's Metaphysics of Free Will, Fall, and Salvation: A 'Divine Comedy' of the Universe," in *Philosophical Essays* (Chicago: University of Chicago Press, 1980), 305–23.

teriality, and how to pass beyond the fall into future spirituality.[5] A journey forward to God is offered to all: souls ascend through various heavens, living and learning in order to become more knowledgeable and balanced. The Hellenistic Egyptian theologian Origen rejected possible successive worlds in time, for successive worlds would imply further falls and negative histories of sin. That model would be incompatible with theologies of the incarnation with the *apocatastasis*, the happy resolution of all intelligences in the Word, who on Earth is the risen Jesus Christ. The end mirrors the beginning.

Angels are powerful beings, vastly different from rational animals on Earth. Some early theologians thought that all of them had some materiality, although in comparison to humans they were quite spiritual.[6] That streak of matter distinguished them from God, for only God could be pure spirit, although their corporeality limiting them in space was matter of an infinite lightness. In the fourth century Christian theologians more and more rejected angelic matter; for Augustine in the fifth century, this was an open question, while a century later Gregory the Great rejected it.

Origen thought that the stars and planets visible in the sky are alive. Each star and each planet is a living body of light and not an angel. These beings, large and spherical, located far from Earth, have a happy life, one of great peace and order. The stars visible in the sky are in no way a menace to human beings; if a few are evil, those are far away. "Like all his contemporaries, Origen thinks that the universe was filled with rational, spiritual beings who had powers and responsibilities which were much greater than anything in the human race. Like his predecessors in Hellenistic philosophy, he divides these

---

5. Origen spoke of "another world" for "the improvement of those who stand in need of it." This is a kind of purgatory and not a further cycle of worlds and redemptions. Origen, *On First Principles* 2.3, p. 83; see Henri Crouzel, *Origen* (San Francisco: Harper and Row, 1989), 205–18.

6. See J. Michl, "Engel IV (christlich)," in *Reallexikon für Antike und Christentum* (Stuttgart: Anton Hiersemann, 1962), 5:121–23; G. Bareille, "Ange d'après les Pères," in *Dictionnaire de théologie catholique* 1:1 (Paris: Letouzey et Ané, 1930), 1195–98; Crouzel, *Origen*, 212. In his opening lines on angels, Thomas Aquinas argued firmly against the idea that these powerful and different creatures have any trace of corporeality, although he knew that some early theologians held this. *Summa Theologiae* I, 50, 1 and 2.

beings into angels and heavenly bodies without making clear how these two groups were related to each other."[7] A personal history of morality somehow combines with a spiritual and metaphysical fall; the arrangements of the stars are caused by the degrees of severity in previous sin. While some intelligences fell slightly and are high angels, the fall of others led them to serve as souls for the bodies of human beings, a race whose inclinations are strongly sensual. The philosophical and religious world of the Hellenistic period looked down on matter and sought to rise to a spiritual life of the mind. Affirming stars to be primal intelligences in fiery forms and planets and the moon to be heavenly material bodies, Origen saw a variety of creatures in a universe where beings of matter and intelligence have a unity of being, fall, and rebirth.[8]

It appears that the divine Word (incarnate in Jesus) has a wider incarnational activity.[9] The preexistent soul of Jesus is the center of all the worlds of intelligences before and after Bethlehem. Teaching and power arrived on Earth with the Word incarnate in Jesus of

---

7. Alan Scott, *Origen and the Life of the Stars: A History of an Idea* (Oxford: Clarendon University Press, 1991), 133. Some theologians in the fourth century had no problem with the divine power creating other worlds or with the existence of intelligent beings in or on heavenly bodies. They were, however, dubious about such ideas due to a commitment to the perspective of one world. See John Chrysostom, *De incomprehensibili Dei natura* 4.2, in *Patrologia Graeca*, vol. 48 (Migne), 729; Athanasius, *Oratio contra gentes* 39, in *Patrologia Graeca*, vol. 25 (Migne), 80; Basil, *In Hexameron, Homilia* 3, 3, in *Patrologia Graeca*, vol. 29 (Migne), 57–58; Ambrose, *In Hexameron* 2.2, in *Patrologia Graeca*, vol. 24 (Migne), 146. Theodore of Scythopolis was a bishop in Galilee in the mid-sixth century. He was an opponent of Origenist theology. In a document addressed to the Emperor Justinian, he condemned ideas associated with Origen or his followers. Among them was the erroneous view that the Word of the Trinity became similar to an angel and existed in various angelic orders. É. Amman, "Théodore de Scythopolis," in *Dictionnaire de théologie catholique* 15 (Paris: Letouzey et Ané, 1946), 286.

8. Crouzel, *Origen*, 209–12.

9. In Origen, the created, temporal preexistence of the soul of Jesus of Nazareth should not be confused with the eternal Word of the Trinity, who in a divinely metaphysical act grounds that human revealer and redeemer. Irenaeus, a Greek-speaking Syrian teaching in Lyons, also saw God's saving history as lengthy and not beginning with Abraham or Jesus.

Nazareth to lead human beings to a higher life away from matter, and his teaching about the reality of sin and redemption through his death and resurrection can serve all in their journey to a cosmic fulfillment.[10] In the universe the Logos (sometimes referred to as "the Christ") works salvation in several forms for several worlds. He is a man for humanity, and he is an angel for each kind of angel. J. A. Lyons writes, "Because Origen holds that angels and men have essentially the same nature and are consequently transformable into one another, his meaning is that the body of the soul united to the Logos acquires an angelic condition among the angels, just as among men it acquires a human condition."[11] Origen gave a cosmic scope to the incarnation. The Logos permeates the risen Christ, and that person can move from nature to nature. "Taking the view that redemption is operative throughout the cosmos, Origen tries to evade the restrictive geocentricism which a unique terrestrial sacrifice seems to impose."[12]

Origen wanted to locate the biblical life and work of Jesus in a salvation history that is a cosmic drama. Incarnation's wide saving action is expressed as a particular event in creatures. The biblical record is a paradigmatic but partial religious cosmology. The gift of redemption and eternal life and the process of incarnation are also extraterrestrial.

Thomas Aquinas (Thirteenth Century)

Thomas Aquinas (1225–74) lived in a time of exploration: the exploration of new ideas and texts, particularly the writings of Aristotle and his Arabic commentators, and the exploration of Asian empires to the East. Active in the new community of universities, Aquinas wrote and taught at the high point of the Middle Ages. His teacher was Albert of Lauingen, who brought together theology and empiri-

---

10. "The crucifixion is twofold: there is Christ's visible sacrifice as a human being for other human beings, and an invisible sacrifice for all of rational creation." Scott, *Origen and the Life of the Stars*, 141.

11. J. A. Lyons, *The Cosmic Christ in Origen and Teilhard de Chardin: A Comparative Study* (Oxford: Oxford University Press, 1982), 139.

12. Ibid., 141.

cal science and defended the autonomy of all the sciences. Dante's great poem, mentioning Albert and Thomas, was an imaginative journey through the realms of the universe.

A millennium after Origen, Aquinas fashioned an original theological system for his cultural age, one formed not by Origen's Middle Platonism but by Aristotelian science. Aristotle rejected an infinite universe and a plurality of worlds, maintaining that the universe was composed of a finite amount of matter where the activity, purpose, and symmetry of nature were central. No matter how numerous the finite entities, the totality remains finite. An infinite universe would lack form, and a universe without a single center would be dysfunctional—and observers on Earth do not see a chaotic or disconnected cosmos. Aquinas also affirmed one universe. A single unity finds support from science as well as from theology, for God the Creator is one.[13] An overarching unity gives place and order to each reality. Aquinas knew of natural philosophers who had posited a number of worlds. He treated the topic of one or many worlds as an issue in metaphysics and physics and not in Christian theology. Cosmologies with many worlds had two problems: first, they located the origin of the universe in chance, and second, they neglected wisdom's order. Plural worlds meant a number of worlds with no single source and with no relationships among the parts.

Is not God's power infinite? Certainly this one cosmos cannot place limits upon God's creativity. Still, God's power has goals other than fashioning worlds. If other worlds are just like ours, they have no purpose: if they are different, this world would be incomplete and poorly conceived. The visible cosmos unfolds as a totality with adequate diversity and unity.[14] In the thirteenth century those arguing

---

13. "A hierarchy in which everything had its relation to the Creator was compatible with the Aristotelian hierarchy of spheres; to introduce other worlds, perhaps with their own bodies and spheres, but necessarily not ordered to our world and the Creator, was to shatter the concepts of unity, perfection, and order." Steven J. Dick, "Aristotelian Natural Law versus Divine Omnipotence," 27.

14. Aquinas, *In Aristotelis De Caelo et Mundo Expositio* (Turin: Marietti, 1952), I, lect. 19, 94. A further argument came from the centrality of Earth with its gravity. "For it is not possible for there to be another earth than this one, because every earth, wherever it might be, would be born by nature to

for a plurality of worlds seem to understand "world" to be exactly like ours, while another world would be "a totality diverse in kind from ours."[15] Aquinas is considering not other units within a single universe much greater than the Ptolemaic system, like a gathering of galaxies, but other universes with no connection to the Milky Way or to each other. Furthermore, he is not enthusiastic about a variety of complex bodies existing with knowing powers; nor does he think that on Earth a second kind of humanity would emerge after the positive climax in the resurrection for the present race.[16]

In looking at Aquinas' theological directions and attempting to think along with him, it is a mistake to stop with this or that conclu-

---

this middle point. And the same reason applies to the other bodies which are parts of the universe." *Summa Theologiae* I, 47, 3 corpus and ad 3. When Peter of Spain was elected pope as John XXI in 1276, the former Parisian professor asked the archbishop of Paris, Stephen Tempier, to look into ideas drawn from Aristotelianism that might be injurious to the faith. A commission came up with 219 propositions, a few of which were close to positions of Aquinas; one of those propositions held that there could be only one world. See Jean-Pierre Torrell, *Saint Thomas Aquinas*, vol. 1, *The Person and His Work* (Washington, DC: Catholic University of America Press, 1996), 298–301; J. F. Wippel, "Thomas Aquinas and the Condemnation of 1277," *The Modern Schoolman* 62 (1995): 233–72.

15. *Summa Theologiae* I, 16, 79. Marie I. George argues that Aquinas would reject the existence of intelligent extraterrestrials in light of his texts about the unity of the universe as understood in the Middle Ages and his critique of Origen's view of stars having souls. Obviously, scientific perspectives in the thirteenth century would differ from many conclusions held by science centuries later. "On the one hand, the human species would reflect God's goodness in a special way by being unique, while, on the other hand, it is befitting to God's goodness that he create more of better creatures. Aquinas leans in the direction of the former view, but realizes that the latter could in fact be the case." George, "Aquinas on Extra-Terrestrial Life," *The Thomist* 65 (2001): 257f.; see George, *Christianity and Extraterrestrials? A Catholic Perspective* (New York: iUniverse, 2005). Rejecting the animation of heavenly bodies is Aquinas, *Summa contra Gentiles* II, 90. He observed that in the astronomical argumentation over whether heavenly bodies are living beings a conclusion one way or another does not pertain to Christian faith; research into the cosmos belongs to science (*Summa contra Gentiles* II, 70).

16. On Aquinas' rejection of a second race on Earth, see *Summa contra Gentiles* IV, 83.

sion from medieval philosophy. The first biographer of that synthetic theologian associated the word "new" with his methods and topics. "In his courses he stated new problems, discovered new methods, and used new sequences of proofs. To hear him teach was to be in contact with a new doctrine supported by new argumentation."[17] Otto Pesch concludes, "Anyone who knows a little of St. Thomas is never safe from making surprising discoveries."[18] A few of Aquinas' principles offer supportive insights for considering extraterrestrials theologically.

God is immaterial and without limits; he is intelligent and eminently active. "Comprehending all in itself, it contains being as an infinite and indeterminate sea of reality."[19] In God are many ideas, ideas for everything that was made, will be made, or that could be made. God is a creator-artist who, out of the ideas of all realities, freely leads forth beings into their actuality.[20] God is not lonely, not alone in the absence of being and time before creation. The divine motive for all God's actions towards beings is goodness. Generosity comes from goodness and is realized in love pouring itself outward by bestowing existence on others. Love carries the divine plans into external realizations. "God is a living fountain, one not diminished in spite of its continuous flow outwards."[21] God intends a universe that is diverse and also coherently empowered. "God has produced things in existence to communicate his goodness to creatures and to

17. William of Tocco, *Ystoria sancti Thomae de Aquino* (Toronto: Pontifical Institute of Medieval Studies, 1996), 121–22, cited in M.-D. Chenu, "S. Thomas Innovateur dans la créativité d'un monde nouveau," in *Tommaso d'Aquino nella Storia del Pensiero: Le Fonti del Pensiero di S. Tommaso* (Naples: Edizioni Domenicane Italiane, 1974), 39–50.

18. Otto-Hermann Pesch, "Thomas Aquinas and Contemporary Theology," in *Contemplating Aquinas: On the Varieties of Interpretation*, ed. Fergus Kerr (London: SCM, 2003), 216.

19. Aquinas, *Summa Theologiae* I, 13, 11.

20. Ibid. I, 14, 8; Aquinas spoke of "the art of divine wisdom and the realm of divine goodness." Ibid. III, 1, 1, 3.

21. Aquinas, *Super Evangelium Ioannis Lectura* (1:4) (Turin: Marietti, 1952), ch. 1, lect. 3, 20. Some commentators on Aquinas in the sixteenth and seventeenth centuries concluded that after creation there is not more being but more beings.

represent that goodness in them. Because it [that goodness] cannot be represented efficaciously by one creature alone, he has created many diverse things so that in various ways what one does not present as from the divine goodness another does."[22]

Intelligent creatures are the summit of the universe; they exist on Earth and in countless spiritual (angelic) forms. Intelligent creatures reflect the divine in a special way; they are the image of God mentioned by Genesis, an image found in the ability to know and to be free.[23] Reason can understand nature; reason can discover how to analyze the causes of things not solely by referring them to the Supreme Cause but in their proper natures. Angels and earthlings are part of a wider polity of divine life, beings with whom God can be friends.[24] Given an emphasis upon higher forms of life, is it not likely that the universe contains a variety of them? Aquinas' voluminous writings are not formally about metaphysics and science but about a shared life with God, something revealed by Jesus. God offers human beings a kind of participation in the divine life. There is a depth and richness in graced life rooted in friendship with the divine persons. "It is not suitable that God provide more for creatures being led by divine love to a natural good than for those creatures to whom that love offers a supernatural good."[25] Each free and knowing person receives this "grace," which brings friendship with God and the seed of a future life in a resurrection from the dead. Creation brings history, and God has entered into history.

The divine motive for creation is God's goodness diffusing itself, and that is also the motive for what is called incarnation. Incarnation means that a divine person (from the community of three) without losing its identity becomes an individual creature. In Jesus of Nazareth, the mission of the Word has a particular intensity: a silent presence of God brings a special grounding of Jesus' reality. "The incarnation was suitable to God because of the infinitely high

---

22. Aquinas, *Summa Theologiae* I, 47, 3. "Consequently it is the entire universe that participates in and represents the goodness of God more than any one creature." Ibid. I, 47, 1.

23. Ibid. I, 93, 4 and 5.

24. Ibid. I, 20, 2, 3.

25. Ibid. I-II, 110, 2.

level of his goodness intent on human salvation."[26] The universe is vast. Is the divine love that seeks intimacy with creatures equally vast?

Did Aquinas think there could be other incarnations? While the Word and Jesus are one, the life of Jesus on Earth does not curtail the divine Word's being and life: "The power of a divine person is infinite and cannot be limited to anything created."[27] All three persons can become incarnate because incarnation is one aspect of an endlessly rich divine power, and so each divine person could be incarnate (beyond Jesus) in further creatures.[28] Aquinas observed that the species of nature, including the human race, have precise properties and these influence the activities of divine grace in the human person. This specificity in nature and grace would be true in other intelligent peoples. A variety of civilizations with billions of persons in the universe suggests a variety in number and in kind of intense relationships with the Trinity.

Guillaume de Vaurouillon (Fifteenth Century)

Guillaume de Vaurouillon[29] (ca.1392–1463) is of particular interest because he addressed directly the theological issues concerning

---

26. Ibid. III, 1, 1, 2. "Texts on the Incarnation, grace, and Trinity confirm the impression that divine love is the synthetic theme that draws into a unity all that Aquinas says as he employs the axiom of good diffusing itself in different ways." Jean-Pierre Jossua, "L'Axiome 'Bonum diffusivum sui' chez S. Thomas d'Aquin," *Revue des sciences religieuses* 40 (1966): 153.

27. Aquinas, *Summa Theologiae* III, 7, 3.

28. "In a new way God unites himself to a creature, or, rather, unites the creature to himself" (Ibid., III, 1, 1, 1). Curiously, Aquinas asked whether the entire universe should have been contacted by one incarnation of the Word. Is not a collective subject more suitable for incarnation than an individual subject, one human being? God's unlimited power could become present variously—in animals and plants—but this would not be meaningful. Much of what is material in the universe has no spiritual soul; the soul is the image of God, and that is the point of entry for an incarnation. Moreover, when God becomes incarnate in a finite person, he does touch the entire universe. In the human person in some way, all of nature flows together (cf. ibid., III, 4, 1 and 4).

29. Vorilongus, Vaurouillon, and Vorrilon are forms of the name; see Ignatius Brady, "William of Vaurouillon, O. Min.," *Miscellanea Melchor de Pobladura,*

extraterrestrials. The topic of whether God could or did create several worlds either simultaneously or temporally was treated by medieval writers in the Franciscan school. They showed more openness to that direction than did the Dominican followers of Aquinas. Bonaventure, biographer of Francis of Assisi and author of speculative and mystical writings, wrote in the thirteenth century that God could have made others worlds: "He was able to make a hundred such worlds, one in a higher place than another, and, still more, one embracing all of them. And too God could make a time before this time and in it make a world."[30]

A Franciscan of the friary of Dinan in Brittany, de Vaurouillon lectured in Paris after 1427 on the *Sentences* of Peter Lombard. After attaining a doctorate and doing some teaching, he attended the Council of Basel in 1433. He began to teach in Paris in 1448. He was the author of commentaries on scholastic systems by Peter Lombard and Duns Scotus, one of which was printed five times in twenty years. "His principles for lecturing on the *Sentences* give access to various issues in scholastic education but at the same time carry a new humanistic spirit which will have some effect on scholasticism."[31] He was interested in history, paid attention to a pedagogical literary style, and treated contemporary issues. His professorships, his presence at Basel, and his role in public disputations led to special praise from Pope Pius II. Michael Crowe refers to him as "the first author who raised the question of whether the idea of a plurality of

vol. 1 (Rome: Institutum Historicum O. F. M. Cap., 1964), 291–315; Franz Pelster, "Wilhelm von Vorillon, ein Skotist des 15. Jahrhunderts," *Franziskanische Studien* 8 (1921): 48–66; Erich Wegerich, "Bio-bibliographische Notizen über Franziskanerlehrer des 15. Jahrhunderts," *Franziskanische Studien* 29 (1942): 195.

30. Bonaventure, *Commentaria in quatuor libros sententiarum*, lib. 1, dist. 44, art. 1, quaest. 4 [*Opera Omnia* 1, 789] (Quaracchi: Collegium S. Bonaventurae, 1882). See Grant McColley and W. H. Miller, "Saint Bonaventure, Francis Mayron, William Vorilong, and the Doctrine of a Plurality of Worlds," *Speculum* 12 (1937): 388–89; on Bonaventure and the Franciscan school, see Ilia Delio, "Franciscan Cosmic Christology," in *Christ in Evolution* (Maryknoll, NY: Orbis, 2008), chap. 3; Delio, "Christ and Extraterrestrial Life," *Theology and Science* 5 (2007): 249–65.

31. Pelster, "Wilhelm von Vorillon, ein Skotist des 15. Jahrhunderts," 48.

worlds is compatible with the central Christian notions of a divine incarnation and redemption."[32]

De Vaurouillon inquired into divine power and limitations. Could not the absolute power of God have created a better world? God could create an infinity of worlds, and indeed an infinity of worlds better than this one. "Infinite worlds, more perfect than this one, lie hid in the mind of God."[33] Each of these worlds would have its own created forms. "It is possible that the species of each of these worlds are different from those of our world."[34] He did not, however, imagine knowledge from those worlds coming to men and women on Earth, for they are too distant; only angelic communication or some special divine action could make us aware of them.[35]

De Vaurouillon looked at the role of Christ in a nuanced way. The theologian considered not only the nature of revelation but also sin and the role of a redeemer on another world. "If it be inquired whether people, existing on that world, have sinned as Adam sinned, I answer, No. They would not have contracted sin just as their humanity is not from Adam."[36] His view of original sin as solely terrestrial removes the need of redemption for other worlds. For another world, Jesus Christ would be somehow a universal figure, although he will not move from planet to planet. "As to the question whether Christ by dying on this Earth could redeem the inhabitants of another world, I answer that he was able to do this not only for our world but for infinite worlds. But it would not be fitting for him to go to another world to die again."[37] There can be other worlds with other creatures; they are not necessarily implicated in our world of sin, do not need a savior, and would not particularly profit by having a savior come from another world. De Vaurouillon's theological distinctions concerning extraterrestrials make him a pioneer;

---

32. Crowe, "A History of the Extraterrestrial Life Debate," *Zygon* 32 (1997): 149.

33. Guillaume de Vaurouillon, *Quattuor librorum Sententiarum Compendium venerabilis patris fratris Guillermi Vorrillonis* lib. 1, dist. xliv (Basel: Langerdorf, 1510), folio 105.

34. Ibid.

35. Ibid.

36. Ibid.

37. Ibid.

he is an intermediary between the scholastics of the thirteenth and fourteenth centuries who declared that God could in theory create a plurality of worlds and the philosophers of science in the sixteenth and later centuries who asserted that God had created such a panoply.

Thinkers from the Middle Ages like Aquinas and de Vaurouillon, although they could not provide much empirical support, offer ideas for a later dialogue between Christian faith and a wider universe.

Renaissance Thinkers
(Fifteenth and Sixteenth Centuries)

To move from the Middle Ages to the late Renaissance is to move into an age of science and observation. Around the same time as de Vaurouillon, in 1440 the influential Nicholas of Cusa (1401–64) in his work *On Learned Ignorance* held for the idea of a plurality of worlds and for the existence of life on the moon and the sun. "We surmise that none of the other regions of the stars is empty of inhabitants."[38] There are no privileged positions for any celestial body; the universe has no center and no boundary. "The Earth is a *noble star* which has a light and a heat and an influence that are distinct from that of all other stars, just as each star differs from each other star with respect to its light, its nature, and its influence."[39] All that is created is equidistantly far and utterly distinct from God; indeed, the vastness of the universe is a visible sign of the infinite, creative power of God. The divine Logos, the second person of the Trinity, present in terrestrial history in Jesus of Nazareth, is indeed divinely transcendent but also immanent in the universe. The Word is present in every star and in every being. It is not a physical centrality that enhances the planet Earth and humans but their relationship to the Creator of the vast universe.[40] Incarnation is intense divine power concentrated in an individual.

38. Nicolaus of Cusa, *On Learned Ignorance*, trans. Jasper Hopkins (Minneapolis: Arthur J. Banning, 1985), II, 12 120.

39. Ibid., II, 12, 118. See Peter J. Casarella, ed., *Cusanus: The Legacy of Learned Ignorance* (Washington, DC: Catholic University of America Press, 2006).

40. Nicolaus of Cusa, *On Learned Ignorance* III, 1-4.

While the Dominicans in the thirteenth century opted for a single ordered world, after the Renaissance, two Dominicans of the late sixteenth century, Tomasso Campanella and Giordano Bruno, held for multiple worlds. Campanella (1568–1634) summoned up passages from early theologians and the Bible to defend a plurality of worlds. Precisely the absence of a discussion in Scripture of a plurality of worlds urges the study of this topic. "If there are humans living on other stars, they would not be infected by the sin of Adam since they are not his descendants. Hence they would not be in need of redemption, unless they suffered from another sin."[41] The Dominican pointed out the limitations of Aquinas' texts: "It must be noted that nowhere in the canons of the Church is there to be found a decree which denies that there are many worlds."[42] The Bible is concerned not with the physics of the universe but with the realm of grace.

Giordano Bruno (1548–1600), born in Nola, not far from Naples, was a member of the Naples Province of the Dominicans like Thomas Aquinas centuries before. He set aside his life of cloistered scholasticism in 1579 to seek his fortune in northern Europe. Metaphysician more than theologian, astronomer but also magician and poet, he lived in academic societies in Geneva, London, and Wittenberg, theological centers where he inevitably aroused hostility and found a lack of intellectual freedom. He established himself in Venice, perhaps because he hoped to find tolerance there and a position at the University of Padua (that chair was twenty years later given to Galileo). Prone to dramatic public statements, he was, contrary to his expectations, arrested in Venice in 1592 and then imprisoned in Rome for several years. He was tried and executed for mainly religious reasons, like the use of magic, his negative views of Jesus' relationship to God and human salvation, his rejection of the Real Presence, and his criticism of the identification of the authority of his Jesuit judge with the life of the church itself. He was not executed

---

41. Tomasso Campanella, *A Defense of Galileo* (Notre Dame: University of Notre Dame Press, 1994), 112. Treating arguments of Aquinas, Campanella notes that for Aquinas the oneness of the universe is a scientific issue; see Frances A. Yates, "Giordano Bruno and Tommaso Campanella," in *Giordano Bruno and the Hermetic Tradition* (Chicago: University of Chicago Press, 1964), 360–97.

42. Campanella, *A Defense of Galileo*, 111.

for his affirmation of an infinite universe nor for his view that there are intelligent creatures elsewhere in the universe.

Bruno taught that the world is infinite and living. The totality is animated and holds many worlds, of which Earth is only one. The stars occupy the pinnacle of a hierarchy of living things, moved by inner principles of life.[43] In addition to this stellar gallery, he proposed that planets and stars are populated with individuals. He was a person of creativity and insight: Johannes Kepler praised Bruno's speculative gifts. Some scholars have thought that he may have wanted to see the entire universe as the second person of the Trinity. Ingrid Rowland notes, "The Nolan philosophy, however, made scant use of calculations or empirical observations. Instead, it relied on mental geometries that are strange to us, and foresaw the need for new kinds of mathematics to account for the conditions of an expanded universe. Bruno's mathematical world is in some respects entirely alien to modern science; in other respects (especially in the recognizably Platonic emphasis of string theory on unity and elegance) it is uncannily familiar."[44]

Campanella and Bruno offered theories on the vastness of the universe and its populations. In a time when science, philosophy, faith, and theology were too intertwined, their lasting contributions got lost in religious eccentricity and ecclesiastical violence.

43. Giordano Bruno, *De l'infinito, universo et mondi* (1584). "[This infinite world] is the true subject and infinite material of the infinite divine actual potency, as this was made well understood both by regulated reason and discourse and by divine revelations which state that there is no count of the ministers of the Most High, to whom thousands of thousands assist and ten hundreds of thousands administer. These are the great animals of which many, with the clear light which emanates from their bodies, are from all sides visible to us." Bruno, *The Ash Wednesday Supper*, dialogue 4 (The Hague: Mouton, 1975), 134.

44. Ingrid R. Rowland, *Giordano Bruno* (New York: Farrar, Strauss and Giroux, 2008), 282. On the subsequent attitudes towards Bruno over four centuries, see Bertrand Levergeois, *Giordano Bruno* (Paris: Fayard, 1995), 511–19; Pasquale Giustiniani et al., eds., *Giordano Bruno: Oltre il mito e le opposte passioni* (Naples: Facoltà teological dell'Italia meridionale, 2002); Luciano Iannaco et al., eds., *Giordano Bruno 1600–2000: Testimone dell'infinito* (Perugia: ali&no, 2004); Maria Elena Severini, *Bibliografia di Giordano Bruno 1951–2000* (Fome: Edizioni die Storia e Letteratura, 2002).

The idea that there are intelligent persons on distant planets is not completely new. A few philosophers and theologians have presumed that such creatures exist. Extraterrestrials are not rivals to people on Earth but expressions of divine power. Sin, person, and grace do not necessarily have the same forms in different worlds, and Jesus, a central figure in Earth's religious history, is not repeatedly incarnate. Time and distance separate one planet from another, and they also separate faiths and religions.

chapter seven

Intelligent Life in the Universe: Perspectives from Christian Thinkers in the Nineteenth and Twentieth Centuries

E picurus and Origen are thinkers far removed from the twenty-first century. In the two recent centuries theological reflection on extraterrestrials has not been absent. In the nineteenth century the debate was heated, and the discussion has continued to have a vitality into the twenty-first century.

Protestant Thinkers
(Reformation to Twentieth Century)

The Protestant Reformation introduced its own perspective on Christian faith, one thoroughly biblical and less drawn from science and metaphysics. Around 1550, the Lutheran systematic theologian Philip Melanchthon warned against the idea that Christ's incarnation and redemption could have occurred more than once. A central Protestant tenet held that salvation came solely from explicit contact with Jesus and with the words of the Bible. "The Son of God is one: our master Jesus Christ, coming forth in this world, died and was resurrected only once. Nor did he manifest himself elsewhere, nor has he died or been resurrected elsewhere. We should not imagine many worlds because we ought not to imagine that Christ died and was risen often; nor should it be thought that in any other world without the knowledge of the Son of God that people would be restored to eternal life."[1] Where Christian faith is centered solely in Jesus of Nazareth, where biblical passages linking Christ to creation are taken to refer to the God-Man without qualification, and where Christian revelation is the sole light for a corrupt humanity, those churches and theologies would have difficulty with the existence of extraterrestrials.

The Enlightenment weakened the Protestant principles of the unique affirmation of the incarnate Word in Jesus and the corrupting force of sin. In the United States in the eighteenth century, liberal religious thinkers and philosophers moved away from Protestant churches in a philosophical, deist direction; they affirmed a benign supreme being and an intelligible universe. For Thomas Paine, the breadth of the universe is filled with creatures in the way that Earth is filled with living beings, and so it is likely that a Supreme Being populates planets. That perspective rendered original sin and a subsequent redemptive incarnation unnecessary. "Are we to suppose that every world in the boundless creation had an Eve, an apple, a serpent, and a redeemer? In this case the person who is irreverently called the Son of God, and sometimes God himself, would have nothing else to do than to travel from world to world, in an endless succession of deaths, with scarcely a momentary interval of life."[2] Paine is stating succinctly some of the contradictions that arise from projecting a simplistic Christology on the entire universe. Ralph Waldo Emerson delivered a sermon in May of 1832 asking how one can be a Calvinist in light of modern astronomy. After stating that the earth is not the center of the universe and realizing that other creatures may not resemble humans, he found it likely that in the

---

1. Philip Melanchthon, *Initia Doctrinae Physicae, Corpus Reformatorum* 13 (Halle: Schwetschke, 1846; Frankfurt: Minerva, 1963), I, 221.

2. Thomas Paine, *The Age of Reason* (Secaucus: Citadel Press, 1974), 90. Around 1755 Immanuel Kant wrote in *Universal Natural History and Theory of the Heavens* that there were a number of galaxies and inhabitants on other planets; those beings were too wise to sin.

universe there are "inhabitants of other worlds."[3] Much of Christianity would need to be left behind, but not the moral law. A new religion teaches no "expiation by Jesus . . . , no mysterious relations to him. It will teach great, plain, eternal truths."[4] To address those involved in physics and philosophy, Christianity should set aside the centrality of atonement even as it retains some (vague) role for Jesus as "the gracious instrument of [God's] bounty to instruct men in the character of God and the true nature of spiritual good."[5]

Religious sects and prophets, mainly Protestant, affirmed extraterrestrials in the nineteenth century. Michael Crowe has explored at length religious perspectives on this topic from the last two centuries.[6] There were various periods in the nineteenth and twentieth centuries. Groups in the 1850s countered the optimistic views of the previous decades; after 1877 the seeming presence on Mars of canals supported a new band of advocates. At the turn of the century astronomers had come to think that intelligent beings might live on "comets or on planets orbiting double or variable stars, and in such objects as the Orion nebula."[7] Thus, both the philosophy of the Anglo-Saxon Enlightenment and American fundamentalist sects affirmed extraterrestrials. Crowe's survey of perspectives after 1700 offers a remarkable list of Americans from Mark Twain to Joseph Smith who hold for extraterrestrials. One of the founders of the Seventh-day Adventist Church, Ellen White, argued in 1890 that the Word of God passing "from star to star, from world to world, superintending all" found sin on Earth and became incarnate to save the human race; this was "a mystery which the sinless intelligences

---

3. Ralph Waldo Emerson, "Sermon CLVII," in *The Complete Sermons of Ralph Waldo Emerson*, vol. 4, ed. Wesley T. Mott (Columbia, MO: University of Missouri Press, 1989), 158.

4. Ibid., 159.

5. Ibid., 159. In 1854 David Brewster published *More Worlds than One: The Creed of the Philosopher and the Hope of the Christian* (New York: Robert Carter, 1854).

6. Michael Crowe, *The Extraterrestrial Life Debate 1750–1900: The Idea of a Plurality of Worlds from Kant to Lowell* (Cambridge: Cambridge University Press, 1986).

7. Crowe, *The Extraterrestrial Life Debate, Antiquity to 1915: A Source Book* (Notre Dame: University of Notre Dame Press, 2008), 520.

of other worlds desired to understand."[8] So in the nineteenth century, new Protestant movements that one might expect to have had a narrow ideology pursued this possibility. "By 1917 more than 140 books dealing with the question of extraterrestrial life had appeared. By 1917, however, the confidence prevalent a century earlier that the universe teems with life had seriously diminished."[9] At that time new calculations led astronomers to conclude that they would have to give up hypotheses implying a large number of planets in the universe. Later, however, with the discovery of multiple galaxies through the construction of more advanced telescopes in the early twentieth century—Yerkes, Wilson, Palomar—interest in the possibility of other intelligent life reappeared.

The Protestant theologian Paul Tillich wrote in 1957 on a topic, he observed, that was avoided by theologians but alive for many people. Toward the end of his three-volume overview, *Systematic Theology*, he asked basic questions: "How to understand the meaning of the symbol 'Christ' in the light of the immensity of the universe, the heliocentric system of planets, the infinitely small part of the universe which man and his history constitute, and the possibility of other 'worlds' in which divine self manifestations may appear and be received. . . . Our basic answer leaves the universe open for possible divine manifestations in other areas or periods of being."[10] Tillich was one of the few theologians from the considerable number of Protestants composing religious systems in the twentieth century who considered the topic. "Incarnation is unique for the special group in which it happens, but it is not unique in the sense that other singular incarnations for other unique worlds are excluded. Man cannot claim to occupy the only possible place for Incarnation."[11]

8. Ellen White, *The Story of Patriarchs and Prophets* (1922; repr., Mountain View, CA: Pacific Press, 1948), 69.

9. Crowe, "A History of the Extraterrestrial Life Debate," *Zygon* 32 (1997): 159.

10. Paul Tillich, *Systematic Theology*, vol. 2 (Chicago: University of Chicago Press, 1957), 95f. See also David Bradnick, "Entropy, the Fall, and Tillich: A Multidisciplinary Approach to Original Sin," *Theology and Science* 7 (2009): 67–83.

11. Tillich, *Systematic Theology*, 2:96.

Catholic Theologians (Early Twentieth Century)

In the last half of the nineteenth century there was a theological consideration of extraterrestrials by Catholic intellectuals. Januarius De Concilio (1836–98) argued for extraterrestrials from the variety and order of the universe. They were intermediate intelligences between humans and angels. A sterile solar system wastes God's powers. Whether those species fell into sin is uncertain.[12] Joseph Pohle, born in the Rhineland in 1852, was a professor of theology and an author of theological textbooks in German and English. After his ordination in Rome and some teaching in England and Germany, he began in 1889 to teach at the newly founded Catholic University of America in Washington, DC. After a few years in Washington, he became in 1894 professor for dogmatic theology at the faculties of Münster and then of Breslau. Already in 1884 he had published *Die Sternenwelten und ihre Bewohner* (Star-worlds and their inhabitants), which became a popular illustrated book (it received a seventh edition in 1922). Pohle's point of departure was neither science fiction nor theology but the array of stars in the sky and their potentiality for change, for evolution. Why would they not have intelligent life? There are analogies between Earth and the planets and stars, and the plurality of terrestrial life-forms argues for other populated worlds. Pohle's book included a history of the issue ranging from ancient Hindus to two Jesuits of the nineteenth century, Angelo Secchi and Carl Braun. Chapters on astronomy looked carefully at planets, particularly at Mars, the sun and moon, and comets, to evaluate their capability for housing life. He also recognized that nebulae and families of comets and stars are not simply individual suns but clusters of stars. "The most effective weapon in arguing for many worlds with living beings is the full analogy between our earth and many other celestial bodies."[13]

12. Januarius De Concilio, *Harmony between Science and Revelation* (New York: Fr. Pustet, 1889).

13. Joseph Pohle, *Die Sternenwelt und ihre Bewohner*, 2nd rev. ed. (Cologne: Bachem, 1899), 11. See J. Gummersbach, "Pohle, Joseph," *Lexikon für Theologie und Kirche*, 2nd ed., vol. 8 (Freiburg: Herder, 1963), 578.

For Pohle, extraterrestrials probably live in a natural state and find therein a natural happiness. There may be further realms of grace or there may not be; there may be sin or an absence of evil. "No reason compels us to extend to other worlds our own sinfulness and to think of them as caught up in evil."[14] The theologian did not project Earth's salvation history onto other planets. "But even when the evils of sin have infected those worlds it does not follow that an incarnation or redemption must have taken place. God has many other means by which to remit guilt."[15] Pohle wondered whether the incarnation occurred on Earth precisely because our world is weak, small, and not particularly significant. That event gave "little Earth" significance in a grander and wider cosmos. There might be greater and more impressive planets and planetary systems that have or need no incarnation. The German theologian's awareness of narrow ecclesiastical attitudes at that time toward astronomy and theology led him to write mainly chapters on science and only a few pages on theological issues. He held that the question of life on other planets is to be settled through science and reason and not by a particular theology. "We cannot avoid the conclusion that the many worlds capable of life, similar to our Earth, call for a major expansion through knowing creatures. In the last analysis, the ultimate goal of the universe leads to this idea."[16]

The 1950s were years in which Catholics were permitted little discussion of new theological topics, and yet they brought further essays on this issue. Noting the new discussion of flying saucers, Domenico Grasso speculated that in the universe there might be "a great number of possible worlds in terms of the intellectual creature."[17] The prominent Spanish Jesuit theologian Joaquin Salaverri published a study of the issue in 1953. He held that supersonic speeds and an increased estimate of the number of stars argue for the possibility of extraterrestrials. A theology of humans as the sole race because of

14. Pohle, *Die Sternenwelt und ihre Bewohner*, 457.

15. Ibid.

16. Ibid., 449. Pohle wrote a study of nature and grace, *Natur und Über-natur* (Cologne: Bachem, 1913).

17. Domenico Grasso, "La teologia et la pluralità dei mondi abitati," *Civiltà Cattolica* 103 (1952): 255, 263.

their sin or because of their needs for humility is not convincing. He puzzled over the centrality of Jesus but observed, amid a consideration of the various relationships of beings on other stars to sin and grace, that God can have several plans.[18] For Angelo Perego, other worlds would reflect God's eternal oneness. Those peoples are not likely to be descendents of Adam, and space travel colonizing stars distant from Earth is not an option. Thus, if they are not descendants of Adam and Eve, there is no sin.[19] Catholic philosophers and theologians up into the 1950s, sometimes drawing on Joseph Pohle, discussed extraterrestrial worlds with their natural and supernatural conditions and future destinies.

Catholic Theologians (Late Twentieth Century)

In the time of theological renewal leading to the 1960s, a few theologians touched on this topic. Charles Davis (1923–99) wrote in 1960 that the immense size of the universe makes extraterrestrials likely. "While Christ as God-man would be higher than any mere creature, we would have to qualify our statements about his primacy and we could not speak in the full sense about the universal significance of his work. Our view of the world in the narrow sense would be Christocentric, but not our view of the universe."[20] Multiple incarnations underscore incarnation on Earth and manifest the Trinity. "We would not know the relationship between the various incarnations nor the divine scheme of things for this universe. The Second Coming of Christ, for example, would not bring about the

18. Joaquin Salaverri, "La possibilidad de seres humanos extra-terrestres ante el dogma católico," *Razón y Fe* 148 (1953): 23–43; the article gives bibiliographical information on other articles from this period.

19. Angelo Perego, "Origine degli esseri razionali estraterreni," *Divus Thomas* (Piacenza) 61 (1958): 22. Reginaldo Francisco reports a conversation between Jean Guitton and Pope Paul VI in which the pope finds reasonable the reality of extraterrestrials and sees how "the universal church" would include more than Earth. "Possibilità di una redenzione cosmica," in *Origini, l'Universo, la Vita, l'intelligenza*, ed. F. Bertola et al. (Padua: Il Poligrafo, 1994), 121–40.

20. Charles Davis, "The Place of Christ," *The Clergy Review* 45 (1960): 713.

end of the world and transformation by itself but as a subordinate factor in some higher scheme."[21] These are, Davis concluded, possibilities in a new and important field for theological reflection.

Pierre Teilhard de Chardin (1881–1955) was an internationally respected paleontologist and Jesuit theologian. An advocate of evolution, he sought to understand and express religious patterns on a cosmic scale. His theology is imaginative and open-ended, but it is also eminently terrestrial and material. He focused on intelligent life on Earth, for he wanted to show its climactic role in evolution. A future Omega Point draws religious and cultural evolution forward.

The Jesuit's principles—evolution, variety, development of complexity with a climax in intelligence—argue for extraterrestrials. Notes written in 1920 for an unpublished article go beyond an anthropocentric position that only terrestrial humanity has intelligent life in the universe. Evolution on Earth has a cosmic context. "The idea of an earth chosen arbitrarily from countless others as the focus of Redemption is one that I cannot accept."[22] Teilhard sought a wider presence of grace not bound to figures on Earth. "The hypothesis of a special revelation, in some millions of centuries to come, teaching the inhabitants of the system of Andromeda that the Word was incarnate on Earth, is just ridiculous. All that I can entertain is the possibility of a multi-aspect Redemption which would be realized on all the stars."[23] Relativity of time, multiple realizations of one reality, existential situations of sin and redemption—Teilhard briefly raises new problems. "The universe is, both on the whole and at each of its points, in a continual tension of organic doubling-back upon itself, and thus of interiorization. . . . For science, life is always under pressure everywhere . . ., and nothing will be able to stop it carrying to the uttermost limit the process from which it has sprung."[24] Evolution toward complexity on Earth supports intelligence elsewhere, and evolution in the galaxies is not simply the explosions of forces

21. Ibid., 715.
22. Teilhard de Chardin, "Fall, Redemption, and Geocentrism," in *Christianity and Evolution* (New York: Harcourt Brace Jovanovich, 1971), 42.
23. Ibid., 44.
24. Teilhard de Chardin, *The Phenomenon of Man* (New York: Harper and Brothers, 1959), 231.

but a movement toward varied stellar bodies, sometimes planets with their unfolding life-forms. Galaxies with their stars are laboratories for forms of life. More than half a century before the discovery of the first exoplanets, Teilhard wrote, "Despite their vastness and splendor, the stars cannot carry the evolution of matter much beyond the atomic series; it is only on the very humble planets, on them alone, that the mysterious ascent of the world into the sphere of high complexity has a change to take place."[25]

Yves Congar (1904–95) was an influential scholar of the forms of the Christian church as they exist in cultural variety throughout its history. For Roman Catholics, he became a pioneer of ecumenism, the reaffirmation of the local bishop, and the communal nature of church tradition. Interestingly, that researcher of medieval texts also wrote on the relationship of believers to other worlds. Pastoral encounters from the exciting years of French Catholicism after World War II led Congar to consider how the Christian faith is challenged by the wider world. He published in 1959 a book on salvation outside of Christianity; an English translation, *The Wide World My Parish: Salvation and Its Problems*, appeared in 1961.[26] Salvation is

---

25. Teilhard de Chardin, "Life and the Planets," in *The Future of Man* (New York: Harper and Row, 1964), 109. "Contrasting viewpoints condition the ways in which Origen and Teilhard deal with the question of cosmic redemption. Origen presents Christ's redemptive work as a transcendent action which gradually through time takes effect in every realm of creation but which, nevertheless, needs to find corporeal expression in a particular place on a particular occasion (that is, on Calvary). Teilhard, on the other hand, looks at the Redemption from within the creative process. It is like a feedback control, supplying a compensating correction to the process in order to bring it to a successful conclusion. Christ's redemption is but a single activity; nevertheless, on the supposition that the universe contains a plurality of inhabited worlds, its presence must be multiplied throughout those worlds. . . . Such a multiplied presence presupposes a multiplicity of incarnation on the part of Christ. . . . New knowledge about the physical cosmos leads to new suggestions about what a fully cosmic redemption entails." J. A. Lyons, *The Cosmic Christ in Origen and Teilhard de Chardin: A Comparative Study* (Oxford: Oxford University Press, 1982), 214.

26. Yves Congar, *The Wide World My Parish: Salvation and Its Problems* (London: Darton, Longman and Todd, 1961). The book's title comes from a phrase of John Wesley, a founder of Methodism: "I look upon the world as my parish." See J.-M. R. Tillard, preface to Cardinal Yves Congar, *Vaste monde ma*

not solely the private state of an introspective individual kneeling in a dim church but a divine dynamic in human lives and communities with their histories and global conversations. That wider view of God's special presence looks at topics like salvation amid other religions, heaven as the goal of history, the end of the world, the resurrection of the body, reincarnation, and extraterrestrials.

God has given us the scientific capabilities to explore the countless stars. Are not persons inhabiting planets elsewhere in the universe a possibility? Revelation in Christ and in the Bible is not about astronomy and holds no information about grace apart from Earth; it teaches that women and men are made in God's image and called to a life of fellowship with him. Biblical references to God's generosity and sovereign activity support the possibility of persons on other planets. If there are other intelligent creatures, knowledge and freedom make them images of God. Their existence, their nature, and their religious condition should not be decided prematurely. They may have been called to a further life of grace, or not. "Revelation being silent on the matter, Christian doctrine leaves us quite free to think that there are, or are not, other inhabited worlds."[27] Earth should not limit divine power. There may well be other incarnations of the divine persons of the Trinity in finite persons.[28]

Like other theologians, Congar noted that the religious condition of extraterrestrials was similar to the question raised in past centuries about the religious condition of peoples who were not Christian. "For Christians, one of the discoveries of this century is the existence of *other spiritual worlds* representing coherent totalities

---

paroisse: *Vérité et dimensions du salut* (Paris: Cerf, 2000), and Thomas O'Meara, "Yves Congar, Theologian of Grace in a Vast World," in *Yves Congar: Theologian of the Church*, ed. Gabriel Flynn (Louvain: Peeters, 2005), 371–400.

27. Congar, *The Wide World My Parish*, 185.

28. Congar spoke of Jesus as the "absolute pinnacle of the whole Universe, whether existing or possible," and yet, if there are other incarnations, Jesus of Nazareth united to the Word of God would not necessarily be superior to all of them (Congar, *The Wide World My Parish*, 188); see Congar, preface to André Feuillet, *Le Christ Sagesse de Dieu après les épitres pauliniennes* (Paris: Gabalda, 1966), 8–11.

of positive values."[29] He applied the globalization and ecumenism of the twentieth century to the universe. Christianity is perhaps one plan of salvation that has been revealed by the Father and realized by the incarnate Word through the Holy Spirit. The cosmos unfolds a new universality in time and space.[30] In these observations Congar, historian of church institutions, speculated on grace in the cosmos.

Karl Rahner (1904–84) in the second half of the twentieth century fashioned a theology both speculative and existential. His approach, one that was subject-centered and also thoroughly historical, looked at dozens of issues in religion and society. In 1964 he published an article in an encyclopedia treating the question of "star-inhabitants." Noting their great distance from us, he suggested that the issue has little to do with our personal existence and history. Extraterrestrials do not inhabit bizarre moons but live in their own worlds—in the modern sense of "world" as a context of social, cultural, and existential forms. Such creatures are "not distinguished in an important way by where they are located in the cosmos" but by "their intellectual subjectivity determining the reality of space and time."[31] The universe points to multiple realizations of matter, and Earth holds countless forms of life in the context of unity and destiny. One cannot begin with dogmatic assertions that God can create only human beings or that all intelligent subjects live in worlds with

29. Congar, "Non-Christian Religions and Christianity," in *Evangelization, Dialogue and Development* (Rome: Gregoriana, 1972), 144. See Thomas Potvin, "Congar's Thought on Salvation outside the Church: Missio ad Gentes," *Science et Esprit* 55 (2003): 139–63.

30. Congar, "Les religions non bibliques sont-elles des médiations de salut?" Ecumenical Institute for Advanced Theological Studies, *Year-Book 1972–1973* (Jerusalem: Tantur, 1973): 101.

31. Karl Rahner, "Sternenbewohner. Theologisch," *Lexikon für Theologie und Kirche* 9 (Freiburg: Herder, 1964), 1061–62. See Rahner, "Landung auf dem Mond," in *Kritisches Wort: Aktuelle Probleme in Kirche und Welt* (Freiburg: Herder, 1970), 233–34. "In our context it is especially worthy of note that the point at which God in a final self-communication irrevocably and definitively lays hold on the totality of the reality created by him is characterized not as spirit but as flesh. This authorizes the Christian to integrate the history of salvation into the history of the cosmos, even when a myriad of questions remain unanswered." Rahner, "Naturwissenschaft und vernünftiger Glaube," *Schriften zur Theologie* 15 (Einsiedeln: Benziger, 1983), 56; translation by the author.

evil. If it is possible that other intelligent forms of life exist in stellar natures, content with the endowments of their species, it is equally or more likely that they too are invited by God's special love. To presume that any and all intelligent creatures in the universe, other than us, are living a life apart from grace "does not do justice to the real and total relationship of God-spirit-grace."[32]

Toward the end of his life, in 1981 the Jesuit theologian wrote a longer reflection concerning the "history of an intelligent being on another celestial body." Preliminary considerations begin with Earth, a small planet revolving in a huge cosmos. "Today the Christian is aware of living on a tiny planet that is part of a system of a particular sun which itself belongs to a galaxy with 300 million stars and is hundreds of thousands of light years broad, a galaxy estimated to be only one among billions in the universe. It is not easy for an individual to see Earth as the reality for which the universe exists. In this cosmos of gigantic dimensions, a size not even able to be imagined, human beings can feel themselves to be little more than an accidental marginal phenomenon."[33] The experience of human contingency has received "an ultimate intensification" in this kind of universe. How does one combine the discoveries of science about cosmic space with the assertions of theology in terms of the importance of the human race? A further challenge is that "the eternal Logos of God who drives forward these billions of galaxies has become a human being on this small planet which is a speck of dust in the universe."[34] The universe is not a celestial house built by God for human beings and their religions. The feeling of vertigo in the cosmos, however, can further religious maturity: an enormous universe leads to an understanding of a greater God, a grasp of what "infinity" might mean.

We should expect that there are beings on other planets who are corporeal and intellectual. In early times religious views of the cosmos went beyond Earth: angels dwell in a heavenly realm. Today the possibility of the development of life to the point of intelligent consciousness cannot be excluded. "It would be excessively anthro-

---

32. Rahner, "Sternenbewohner. Theologisch," 1062.
33. Rahner, "Naturwissenschaft und vernünftiger Glaube," 56.
34. Ibid.

pomorphic to view the Creator-God as directing cosmic evolution at another location in the universe to the point where the immediate possibility of free and intellectual life is present but then casually breaking off that development."[35] For Rahner, the active, self-seeking person draws forth from God a richer contact. Would there be for each civilization of extraterrestrials revelation and grace as the special self-communication of God? "We presuppose, therefore, that the goal of the world consists in God's communicating himself to it. We presuppose that the whole dynamism which God has instituted at the very heart of the world's becoming by its self-transcendence (but beyond what constitutes nature) is always meant as the beginning and first step toward this divine self-communication."[36] Are intelligent beings normally or always invited to God's special friendship? Rahner expects that special presence of grace to come to others even as he recognizes religious independence in other worlds. "One could say that these other corporeal and intelligent creatures in a meaningful way also have a supernatural determination within an immediacy to God (despite the totally unmerited reality of grace). At the same time we can conclude nothing about the history of freedom of these creatures."[37] Does the evolution of an intellectual being along with shared divine life lead to incarnation? "In terms of the immutability of God in God-self and in the selfhood of the Logos one certainly cannot prove that a pluriform incarnation in various histories of salvation is simply inconceivable."[38]

God is free to fashion other worlds, worlds of different types. From the point of view of theology, there is no veto against a history of free intelligence on another planet. "A theologian can hardly say more about this issue than to indicate that Christian revelation has as its goal the salvation of the human race; it does not give answers to questions which do not in an important way actually touch the

35. Ibid., 58.
36. Rahner, "Christology within an Evolutionary View," *Theological Investigations* 5 (Baltimore: Helicon, 1966), 173.
37. Rahner, "Naturwissenschaft und vernünftiger Glaube," 59.
38. Ibid.

realization of this salvation in freedom."³⁹ A Christian understanding of personal subjectivity and revelation affirms that both matter and spirit aim at development and self-transcendence. What we call grace leads them further. That dynamic bringing together intelligence, matter, and divine presence may find realization in multiple ways in the galaxies.⁴⁰

39. Ibid. See Bela Weissmahr, "Die von Karl Rahner herausgestellte Affinität von evolutiver Weltanschauung und christlichem Glauben," in *Die philosophischen Quellen der Theologie Karl Rahners*, ed. H. Schöndorf (Freiburg: Herder, 2005), 175–80; Phillip Geister, *Aufhebung zur Eigentlichkeit: Zur Problematik kosmologischer Eschatologie in der Theologie Karl Rahners* (Uppsala: Uppsala University Press, 1996), 119–21; Harald Fritsch, "Vollendung des Comos," in *Vollendende Selbstmitteilung Gottes und seine Schöpfung: Die Eschatologie Karl Rahners* (Würzburg: Echter, 2006), 508–511; Denis Edwards, "Resurrection of the Body and Transformation of the Universe in the Theology of Karl Rahner," *Philosophy and Theology* 18 (2006): 357–83; Michael W. Petty, *A Faith That Loves the Earth: The Ecological Theology of Karl Rahner* (Lanham: University Press of America, 1996); Leo O'Donovan, "Making Heaven and Earth: Catholic Theology's Search for a Unified View of Nature and History," in *Theology and Discovery: Essays in Honor of Karl Rahner, S.J.*, ed. William J. Kelly (Milwaukee: Marquette University Press, 1980), 269–99.

40. In the 1980s Hans Küng wrote that one must "allow for living beings, intelligent—although quite different—living beings, also on other stars of the immense universe" (*Eternal Life?* [New York: Doubleday, 1988], 224), but recently he became less positive: "More and more astronomers are now accepting the view that isolated civilizations exist all over the universe between the glowing 'fixed stars' on planets dispersed from one another like grains of sand. Indeed, a whole science and industry developed on the basis of this impulse to make contact with one of the supposed extraterrestrial civilizations. Countless films (such as *ET*), TV shows, popular publications, and scientific enterprises of all kinds were produced on the basis of this hypothesis—not to mention all the attempts to trap radio signals from possible planets of other stars or to send out signals of their own. What was the result? . . . All the attempts were unsuccessful. No one from a distant planet has made any contact with us Earth dwellers that is scientifically demonstrable—not to mention hostile or peaceful extraterrestrial visitors on our Earth. Rather, the most recent space research has shown the opposite: complex life on other planets and their moons is highly improbable" (*The Beginning of All Things: Science and Religion* [Grand Rapids: Eerdmans, 2007], 133). The Swiss theologian's conclusion came before the discovery of hundreds of exoplanets.

✦ ✦ ✦

Historian Michael Crowe concludes his survey of theories about extraterrestrials in modern times thus:

> During the twentieth century the universe expanded at a remark-able rate, became filled with other galaxies, and, as we began to confirm only in 1995, other solar systems. Thus the locales avail-able for extraterrestrials have increased, as have our knowledge of the universe and the power of our telescopic equipment. Were the authors [of recent centuries] to return to life in the twentieth-first century, they would find an area known for over twenty centuries as the plurality of worlds transformed in techniques and title. More-over, astrobiology (the newest title) is pursued by thousands of scientists, enriched in tens of thousand of publications, and funded by many millions of dollars. Although the ultimate answer as yet eludes our efforts, many areas of the debate have seen astonishing progress.[41]

Theologians in antiquity were stimulated by Hellenistic phi-losophy and science to hypothesize life elsewhere in the cosmos. Modern themes like evolution, history, and the subject's existential world have influenced theologians in the past century to consider extraterrestrials in their relationship to life and fulfillment. If there is on Earth a world of grace, there may be on many distant planets cultures of creativity and love, schools of astrobiology and theology.

41. Crowe, *The Extraterrestrial Life Debate, Antiquity to 1915: A Source Book*, 521.

chapter eight

Star-Mentors and Star-Friends

The light coming from the center of our galaxy and reaching Earth tonight has been en route for millions of years. Nicolas Cheetham narrates that journey:

> Tonight the light of an ancient supernova will finally reach Earth. . . . For millions of years, this luminous conflagration has surged across the universe, carried on a wave of photons traveling at 300,000 kilometers per second (186,000 miles per second). Century by century, decade by decade, year by year, it has relentlessly plowed towards us. . . . Traveling 5.9 million miles a year, there is no swifter messenger for vital information, but the immense scale of the universe dwarfs even light's velocity, imposing a communication lag between all cosmic events and ourselves. By the time the light of an extragalactic supernova reaches us, entire stellar generations will have passed away in its home galaxy.[1]

The black winter sky sets off the moon, planets, and stars of varying luminosity, and yet little of the expanding universe is visible to the human eye. Unaided, the human eye can see only some thousands of the universe's trillions of stars. Moreover, contact with

---

1. Nicolas Cheetham, *Universe: A Journey from Earth to the Edge of the Cosmos* (London: Smith-Davies, 2005), 6f.

the universe today comes not only through light and telescopes. Radio waves too manifest galactic objects and forces. "Only in the last century have we become aware of light's many guises and been able to step into this unseen realm—it is no coincidence that our exploration of space has advanced hand in hand with our exploration of the electromagnetic spectrum."[2]

When we know something or learn something, it seems as if in our mind that reality and its context are illumined. We say, "I see." Light puts us in touch with the universe, close and far. God creates light first so that the rest of creation can appear, can be seen. The book of Genesis speaks of the creation of light as a joyful event. In Franz Joseph Haydn's oratorio *The Creation*, the opening line "Let there be light" resounds from chorus and orchestra in C major. Inspired by the roles light plays in the universe, some religious thinkers have affirmed that God is close to light. A letter to Paul's disciple Timothy in the New Testament proclaims that God "dwells in inapproachable light" (1 Tim 6:16), and Thomas Aquinas said that "in the human personality there is the light of reason and the light of grace that shares in God's life."[3] The speed of light is a framework for all of reality. Explosions light-years across aim at creative order; the most intense heat and pressure is in fact a nursery; the speed of light orders all. The light of stars invites the light of minds to explore. Ken Croswell concludes his study: "Is it mere coincidence that the universe happens to possess just those properties which allow part of it to be alive? . . . [Some people] see the universe's remarkable offspring as a sign that an intelligent creator wrote a tremendous symphony whose melodies the stars, galaxies, and planets now play with beauty and precision, and we living beings are one of the fortunate resulting chords, perhaps the climactic chord in that symphony's greatest movement. Whatever the case, and vast and complex though the universe is, its most astonishing features are two of the simplest: it exists, and so do we."[4] It is likely that other civilizations exist, similar to and different from us.

2. Ibid., 7.

3. Aquinas, *Summa Theologiae* I-II, 110, 3.

4. Croswell, *Planet Quest: The Epic Discovery of Alien Solar Systems* (New York: Free Press, 1997), 247.

This book began in an atmosphere of reaction—a reaction to an unnerving question about "aliens." The number of stars and the recent discovery of exoplanets show research moving into truly new areas. Possibility becomes probability. Beyond catalogues of billions of visible stars, some like our sun, there may still be galaxies of suns too far away for their light to reach us. Even those unseen galaxies may be populated with creatures of intelligence.

Looking up at the Milky Way, learning of clusters of stars, the reality of other planets may make someone on Earth feel small. So many stars burn above one fragile life. A second uneasiness, however, has emerged from these pages, a further challenge. The shock is not that somewhere one strange-looking race of intelligent creatures might exist. There would seem to be many populations of intelligence. If there are billions of galaxies each with billions of stars, the chances are that hundreds of thousands of planets have civilizations. They are not all existing now: some have come and gone, fading away into God's providence hundreds of millions of years ago. Others will begin to exist far in the future. Still, thousands of civilizations might live in our space and time. Like a theme arising from a large orchestra with a constant crescendo, the cosmos resounds with the motif of "the More."

We on Earth find for this new journey mentors around us, star-mentors. There are astronomers and astrophysicists, mathematicians and extrobiologists, experts in technology and theologians; there are novelists, poets, and stellar photographers; there are amateur astronomers and essayists. All assist in the conversation between science and religion and contribute to exploring the cosmos. We can include them in what Rainer Maria Rilke wrote of poets and philosophers as voices in history: "One forgets repeatedly that the true philosopher, like the poet, is the bearer of futures among us. Rather than sharing much in their own time, they are the contemporaries of people far in the future and have no reason to trouble people of today. They have a daring progress tempered only by the struggle of going beyond the tremblings of this age and of yesterday; they are the masters of a thousand developments, able in a sovereign way to follow the nuances of these paths."[5]

5. Rilke, *Die Verwandlung der Welt ins Herrliche: Über Kunst und Glück*, ed. Ulrich Baer (Frankfurt: Insel, 2006), 76; translation by the author.

Sciences researching the universe do not need directions from religious faith. Yet science may learn from revelation to look for synthesis and purpose—and to expect tranquil life in the future. For the beginning, progress, or end of the universe, Christian theologians do not favor one physical model over another. They refer to God, but not to a god as a collective being, a judge, or a remote causality. The true God is a person of wisdom and love. Believers also must learn. One cannot afford to remain within a provincial or fundamentalistic faith; one must give up locating religion in magic, superstition, or sanctimonious denunciations. Faith has always had a cosmic dimension. Religion has always been interested in the extent and the future of what is seen in creation. The universe is intricate and beautiful.[6]

What do extraterrestrials mean for us on Earth? There is no reason to think that extraterrestrials are normally hostile. Probably they are called to deeper love and life with God. Star-companions to us in space and time, their intelligences have their own gifts. Do some planets exist in galactic communities? Some are engaged perhaps in technologically complicated dialogues over great distances. The likelihood of extraterrestrials, star-friends, cannot but modify mind and art, existence and technology on Earth. Becoming part of our world whether in theory or reality, they make us think differently about who we are and about what it means to be intelligent and creative. They imply new horizons for the future. New theologies await. Even a revelation believed to come from God would be expanded.

Extraterrestrial peoples—their probability is a discovery. Their intimation is a gift: more life, more art, more science, more revelation.

---

6. Christian de Duve concludes: "Priests are still needed, as are thinkers, scientists, philosophers, poets, writers, musicians, sculptors, painters and other artists. . . . We need priests—or better said, *spiritual guides* so as to avoid the pomp of robes and rites that surrounds the historical image of the priest—to serve as mentors who, without dogmatism or fundamentalism, can inspire, help, and orient." *Life Evolving: Molecules, Mind, and Meaning* (Oxford: Oxford University Press, 2002), 306.

Index of Names